ADRIFT IN SEARCH
OF CAMELLIAS

ADRIFT IN SEARCH OF CAMELLIAS

JUSTIN WONHO CHO

NEW DEGREE PRESS

COPYRIGHT © 2021 JUSTIN WONHO CHO

All rights reserved.

ADRIFT IN SEARCH OF CAMELLIAS

ISBN   978-1-63730-703-8   *Paperback*
       978-1-63730-794-6   *Kindle Ebook*
       979-8-88504-012-9   *Ebook*

CONTENTS

ACKNOWLEDGMENTS

When I began this long journey, I had no idea what I was getting myself into. There were many highs and lows along the way, accomplishments which I will take great pride in and mistakes which I will forever regret. I've discovered so much about myself writing *Adrift in Search of Camellias*, and I am so grateful for all the support. Fulfilling this dream would not have been possible without you.

Thank you first and foremost to my family for supporting me through every step of the way:

Young-rae Cho, Na-Young Kwon

This novel was made feasible primarily through the help of numerous supporters. Thank you so much to everyone who believed in me.

Abigail Cozza	Benjamin Hadler
Adam Syed	Brandon Chien
Adarsh Hullahalli	Brooklyn Robinson
Alex Aragon	Cailin Lin
Andrew Lin	Catherine Santa Presca
Andy Young	Chanyeong Kim
Awais Arshad	Dalton Dickon
Baillie Robinson	David Keet
Balmore B Giron	Dustin Nguyen

Eric Koester
Erica Yuk
Ethan Tan
Eunhae Park-hyun
Garren J Ferreira
Hailey Ko
Heejin Lee
Hyeon Jung Ha
Isabelle Chyun
Jacob E Branscum
Jasmine Tocki
Joon Jin Song
Joshua Michael Hoang
Juan Ignacio Calderon
Julia Hill
Keegan Oster
Kevin Lee
Kihyun Jo
Konami W Masui
Kristopher Chen
Krystle Moos
Kyle Lou
Kyunghee Lee
Larry Song
Laurence D'Ercole
Lisa Beers
Macy Lu
Manasi Ramadurgum
Marius Huhnke
Matthew Misogas
Michael Sheahan
Milena Salazar

Minh Le
Minsun Kim
Mirang Kim
Nami Kwon
Nathaniel Rowe
Nayoung Kwon
Nivedh Neelamkavil
Paula Juhn
Peter Le
Peter Yong
Pragat Muthu
Rachel Elizabeth Langford
Ryan Chhong
Santisouk Truong
Scott Phillips
Sejung Park
Seo-Jun Yun
Seok Yun Lim
Shawn Kim
Sisy Chen
Soon Nan Chang
Sophia Zhao
Sunmi Lee
Sunny Bounyalath
Suyoung Lim
Tejas Saboo
Vincent Casciani
Warren Chang
Yang Ja Choi
Yifan Lin
Young Rae Cho
Younghee Kwon

CHAPTER 1

The sour odor of booze and sweat lingered in the air of the sleazy Austin nightclub. The shrieks and howls of dancers were muddled by the music's deafening bass. At the edge of the club, Jin was sitting with his friend Ethan and a middle-aged alcoholic they'd just met.

Suddenly, a shot glass was slammed on the table.

"Look kid, how do you expect me to put my money into somebody who's a waste of space?" the drunkard barked.

Jin stared blankly at the rough, shabby man before him. He was dressed in an olive cargo jacket that looked like it hadn't been washed in months. His sideburns were long and greasy, and his sunburned skin was an intense orange. The man's presence made Jin feel out of place. Here were two teenagers wearing hoodies and jeans, talking to a grown-ass man.

"C'mon, don't say that about my boy," Ethan said, clasping his hands and maintaining a playful voice. "He might've had a bit of a hiccup, but he's on the come up now. Wouldn't you want to invest now while everyone's busy wasting their time with top competitors? You won't make much money only betting on safe picks."

The man shook his head, leaning back into his booth's seat and lighting a cigar. "You're saying this kid dropped out of middle school and has never had a real job, but you want me to bet on him for VMA nationals?"

Jin held his breath, but the words didn't hurt as much as he thought they would. He'd heard this kind of thing before. Virtual Martial Arts was an online VR sport which had made waves in the eSports scene. It was all he had, but he sucked at it.

He looked down at the disgusting half-drunk Negroni in front of him. Beside him, Ethan had already finished his Dark 'n' Stormy and the man was sipping a bourbon. Jin hated the taste of alcohol. However, he was still tempted to wash down the man's sharp words with a sip.

Ethan shrugged. "What does his education have to do with VMA?"

"Competence. It's about competence." The man took a deep hit of his cigar and blew the smoke at the boys as if they weren't there. "Welcome to the adult world. Money isn't just money, it's an investment. How can I invest in someone if I don't even think they're competent enough to graduate middle school?"

Ethan clenched his jaw but stayed silent. Jin was surprised. Last time something like this happened, Ethan went on a whole rant about judging people off of surface-level details.

The man continued. "Kids like y'all are a dime a dozen. Love to talk but barely have any results or talent to show for. All it takes is for y'all to qualify for nationals once and now suddenly all this confidence comes out."

Jin didn't really disagree with this. He'd tagged along with Ethan to this club, but he wasn't really sure how he thought he could convince a grown man to bet on them, let alone what they'd gain if they actually pulled it off.

Ethan gathered his breath before speaking. "Well, let's talk concrete results then. Why don't you look up our profiles?"

The man tilted his head. He seemed caught off guard. It was a fair proposal. VMA results were public on the VR Association's website, and if there was anything to accurately predict future success, it was past success.

"Fine." The man reached into his pocket and pulled out his smartphone. He leaned on his hand and looked up. "You, uhhh, Jin. What's your last name?"

"Yi. But my full first name is Seokjin. You'll have to use that for my official profile."

He raised his brow. "Chinese or Korean?"

"Korean."

The drunkard smirked. "I used to have a girl who was Korean."

Silence. Jin almost cringed.

When the website's search bar spit out Jin's profile, the man took a quick scan of the page before putting his phone down and reaching for his drink. "Exactly, nothing to take seriously."

Ethan lowered his head, looking defeated. Jin wasn't sure why Ethan was expecting any other response. He was in the middle of a seven-game losing streak—of course this guy wouldn't bet on him. However, it still hurt to see his friend with that kind of face.

"Check his next," Jin said.

The man stirred his glass, watching the ice cubes spin. "Why waste my time, kid?"

"I think you'll be surprised." Jin looked the man straight in the eye, perhaps for the first time since they'd begun talking.

The man peered back with a straight face. He paused before unlocking his phone again and turned toward Ethan. "What's your name?"

Ethan hesitated, as if he wasn't expecting the conversation to turn to him. Again, Jin wasn't sure why. If Ethan really wanted bets, he would be the obvious favorite: he was last year's Texas state champion.

"Ethan Miller," he finally said.

"I thought you were a chink like your friend? That's not really an Asian-sounding name," the man said as he typed.

"Dad gave me the name. He's white. I got the looks from my mom."

"A mixed blood, huh. So y'all rea—" The man paused. He lifted his phone to eye-level and looked back and forth between Ethan and the screen, as if to confirm that the boy in the profile picture was indeed the same boy sitting in front of him. His eyes widened. "Now look what we have here. Maybe there is some competence."

Ethan chuckled, but he didn't seem very happy.

The man chuckled back before catching himself. Another pause. He leaned in closer to his screen and squinted. "Wait, you're only seventeen?"

Ethan's face twisted, trying to think of a response.

The man shook his head and yanked his bag from beside him. "What the fuck am I doing drinking with a bunch of minors? Y'all shouldn't even be here." He stormed away, leaving his drink half sipped on the table.

There was an uncomfortable stillness amid the deafening music.

Suddenly, Ethan snatched the man's drink and gulped it down. "SHIT."

Jin grinned. This was their second rejection. Perhaps if he was with anyone else, this would've felt like a waste of time, but ever since they were kids, there was something about Ethan's carefree demeanor that always managed to amuse him. So when Ethan told him earlier that day that he wanted to celebrate their qualification to nationals by going to a club and finding people who'd bet on them, he just laughed. "The trick is to find the desperate, dirty looking people. If they look like they have their life together, they won't fork down any money," Ethan had said.

None of the trashy clubs in the area cared enough to ID, so they definitely could get in, but no reasonable adult would bet on a bunch of kids. Their efforts would pretty much always end up like, well, what just happened. It was stupid, like the rest of Ethan's plans. Jin was sure that Ethan secretly knew his ideas would never work. But that was what made it so fun.

After a moment, Ethan stood up and stretched his arms. "Fuck it, another one?"

Jin stood up as well. "Let me get some fresh air first."

"All right, just come back soon. I'll look for our next target."

Jin gave a quick nod. He circled around the dance floor, clinging to the wall and occasionally forcing himself through a tight crowd of clubbers.

When he finally made his way out the door, he looked around and saw the dark city illuminated by bright signs advertising various bars, clubs, and restaurants. The chilly evening tickled his skin, and the air already began to reek less of alcohol and cigarettes.

He liked downtown Austin. There was a restless, noisy energy that made the city feel alive. It was a good contrast from his usual quiet routine at his suburban house in Bezo, and it was certainly worth the hour-long train ride. He needed changes in environment like this; long periods without it made him lose track of time as his days blended together.

He would probably go more often if Ethan had more free time. He usually preferred going with Ethan because he was afraid of interacting with strangers alone, but Ethan was a surprisingly busy guy.

Outside, the fresh air and relative serenity was calming. Jin didn't want to go back inside the club. A bigger break couldn't hurt. He wandered through the streets for a while, glancing at the other clubs and bars on the street until a sign caught his attention.

VR ARCADE.

The building was on a corner, shorter than the buildings around it. He didn't know much about arcades, but he knew they were prevalent in the early days of video games. Jin found himself walking inside and found an array of VR stations organized in long rows.

A VR headset was technically all you needed to play most VR games. It was composed of a small monitor, which rested in front of the player's eyes, and a head strap, which locked the monitor in place. Many came with some sort of controller that users held in their hands. Together, these pieces allowed users to move with their physical body and have their virtual avatar make the exact same movements in a VR space.

Many bigger VR sports, however, were designed to be played on a VR station. Stations often looked like a mechanical chair with a headset protruding from the top, and they offered a more complete virtual experience. Instead of simply displaying the virtual space with a monitor, the station's headset completely transferred a player's consciousness into their virtual avatar, leaving their physical body sitting still in the seat.

The VR Arcade's stations were hooked up in pairs with a monitor between each seat to display the current game for spectators. They were organized into rows by sport. Roaming through the aisles, Jin saw various sports such as basketball, racing, and fencing. However, he eventually found what he was looking for: VMA.

It was a simple sport—pick a weapon and fight. The options were brass knuckles, an iron rod, and a spear. First person to drop their opponent's health meter to zero wins. Players could materialize a shield on their arms and legs. If you anticipated a shield, you could make any attack a shieldbreaker, which could pierce through a shield for extra damage. However, if you missed an SB, your body became unmovably heavy for a moment, leaving you open to get hit.

Jin had been competing in VR Fighting tournaments since he was a kid. And now that he was no longer in school, it was all he had.

For some reason, the arcade's VMA section was rather small, and there was only one fight going on. A brief glance at the match was all Jin needed to know that the two players were amateurs with little training. They had strange form and inefficient striking habits. If Jin ever fought like that in front of his coach, Arby, he'd get yelled at.

He didn't want to waste too much time before going back to Ethan, but he couldn't help but watch. VMA always drew him in.

When they finished playing, the two players disconnected. One was tall with brown hair and the other was a small blond. They chatted for a moment before turning toward Jin.

"Do you want to play?" the blond boy asked.

Jin froze. He realized that he'd just been standing around staring. He completely forgot that he was in the presence of strangers. His muscles tensed as the silence grew longer and longer.

I have to respond now, or it'll be weird. Where was Ethan when you needed him? The silence felt like it lasted an eternity before Jin finally jerked his head into a nod.

The boy smiled. "What's your name?"

His voice was gentle. Jin could tell he was a nice guy, but he couldn't stop his heart from pounding.

"It's…uh…Seokjin."

"Oh cool, I'm—"

"But um," he blurted. "Sorry…well…call me Jin."

The boy smiled again before continuing. "Okay, nice to meet you, Jin. I'm Joseph and this is my friend Jorge." He signaled to his side as Jorge waved.

Jin slowly raised his hand and stiffly waved back.

"It's always cool to see other VMA players," Joseph said, scratching the back of his head. "There aren't a whole lot of fighters in this part of town. You want to play a quick match?"

Jorge got up from his seat and signaled toward it, as if to say "here you go."

Hesitation. Jin didn't want to leave Ethan for too long, but he was also tempted to get a quick game in. He didn't know what to do. His mouth began to feel dry. Two nice guys were before him, waiting on a response, but he didn't want to say anything.

"Sure," Jin's mouth said on its own.

"Great," Joseph responded cheerfully, completely ignoring the awkwardness. He turned around to hook up, and Jin followed.

On the station's chair, Jin slid the headset over his eyes to see the usual player interface in the monitor. He used the buttons on the arm of the chair to select "play."

Once connected, he saw the familiar white octagonal floor surrounded by a black cage. The floor was cold against his feet. The blank scent of virtual reality filled his lungs.

Soon, his opponent blinked into existence on the other side. Joseph's broad silhouette looked great in the tight blue material that covered a player's whole body in VMA. Now that it was just them, it was also clear that he was a few inches taller. Jin felt painfully average in comparison.

PICK YOUR WEAPONS! The virtual announcer's booming voice rang through Jin's ears. He chose the iron bar. The boy picked brass knuckles, a weapon with one of the shortest ranges but highest power.

Once the players made their selections, the health meter above the boys' heads appeared, 50-50. The announcer soon started the countdown.

Three, two, one… GO!

The words echoed through the stadium.

Joseph came running off the starting line to begin attacking.

A jab.

A jab.

A straight.

A roundhouse kick.

A jab.

A jab.

A straight.

A—

Predictable.

Jin shielded the kick and smacked the boy's shoulder.

He stood his ground and came running again.

A jab.

A straight.

A jab.

A strai—

Still predictable.

Jin sidestepped and cracked the iron bar straight into the boy's head. He fumbled back, nearly running into the wall behind him. Jin's grip tightened, feeling the coarse rubber of his weapon's grip in his fingers. This was the time to get all over Joseph. He went in again.

Whack. Whack. Whack.

This was it—Jin was clearly winning.

Then suddenly, a counter. The brass knuckles dug into Jin's cheek as the punch connected. He'd made a mistake and let an attack through.

Don't lose, Jin.

The words echoed in his mind and gradually became a chant.

Don't lose, Jin. Don't lose, Jin. Don't lose, Jin. Don't lose, Jin.

Before he knew it, he was there again, in the dark ocean of his mind.

This always happened these days.

He wanted to leave. He needed to leave. But how could he? His limbs felt as tight and rigid as if they were paralyzed, yet they were still moving on their own. He knew these movements. He recognized them, his stance, his strike, his shield, and his kick. However, it didn't feel like him who was making them.

Everything felt dull. His body moved, only to feel no power or return after the strike. He became restless, frantic to feel something. He pushed and pushed and pushed as if he were pounding piano keys, only to hear and feel nothing under his fingers.

He wanted to leave. He needed to leave. Why did this always happen? What did he have to do? What did he do to deserve this?

And just like that, an uppercut to the jaw. The match was already over. Jin had lost.

CHAPTER 2

Why are you still stuck? What are you going to do? Why are you still stuck? What are you going to do?

The words rang through Jin's head. The words were pitch black. They were sharp, cutting deep into his skin as they gripped his throat. His chest tightened. The air began to taste bitter.

Suddenly, Jin's eyes snapped open. He was staring at the ceiling, lying in a nest of cords on the floor. Beside him sat the VR station they were connected to.

"You awake, buddy?" A familiar chirpy voice.

Jin turned his head and saw Arby, his VMA coach, making a coffee by the window. "You fell asleep while practicing last night."

"I see." Jin rubbed his neck—they were still intact. He put his hand on his chest as he breathed, feeling his lungs inflate with air. He slowly got up, feeling some of the tangled wires rise with him. He could feel his messy black hair sticking out in various directions.

Last night, after leaving the club with Ethan, Jin went to the VMA club to practice a bit. He didn't remember falling asleep.

"You must've been really tired," Arby said, chuckling. He was a middle-aged man with an unshaved face and graying hair that was usually combed back. He often spoke aggressively and had a nasty case of coach belly. "You rolled off the chair but just kept sleeping."

"Damn, did I really?"

"Would I lie to you?"

Arby lived in the bedroom on the second floor of his VMA club. Jin came often whenever he had nothing better to do. Arby gave him a key so he could practice whenever. The club was like a second home to him, and Arby was like a second father. He taught him most of what he knew about VMA, life, and philosophy. In many ways, he was more of father to Jin than his real one. His real dad was never in the house.

"I guess not," Jin muttered. He checked the time on his phone—10:39 a.m. It was a Saturday, meaning that Ethan didn't have school. Jin usually tried to visit whenever he could.

"I have to go, Coach. I'm gonna visit Ethan."

Arby had already finished his coffee and was walking upstairs. "Have fun, kid."

Jin waved goodbye and went to the bathroom to wash his face. He brushed his teeth with his spare toothbrush and grabbed a drink of water from the kitchen. He took off his hoodie and stuffed it in his bag. He'd been wearing it since last night, and the Texas sun was always blazing hot in the morning. Once ready, he walked out the door and onto the street.

When he reached Ethan's family's signature flower garden, he knew he was at the right house. It was only a few blocks away from Arby's. The greenery was neatly organized in rows of roses, tulips, and other colorful flowers Jin didn't recognize. He'd seen the garden hundreds of times now and didn't particularly care for flowers, but it always caught his eye for some reason. It was just so vibrant and pristine. There just wasn't anything else like it in all of Bezo. There probably weren't even any if you drove an hour out to Austin. It had always been the pride of the family.

His legs were beginning to get tired, but he managed to drag himself up the familiar steps to Ethan's house and knock on the front door.

"Coming!" Ethan's mother, Mrs. Zhao, called from the kitchen.

The door opened to reveal Mrs. Zhao with a bright smile. "Oh Jin! Come in, you're just in time for breakfa—Oh my! You look terrible? Did something happen?"

Jin chuckled, drawing attention to baggy eyes and messy black hair. "It's nothing, I just fell off a chair in my sleep."

She frowned. "Well that's not good. Anyhow, come in and eat up!"

Mrs. Zhao was a chatty Asian woman who always seemed to be tie her black hair into a tidy ponytail. Even standing completely straight, she only came up to around Jin's shoulders, but he was still occasionally intimidated by her aura. Despite her soft exterior, she carried a vicious side ready to snap at any moment, a trigger that commanded respect. Jin was scared that talking back to her would mean declaring war.

Although Mrs. Zhao was a little intimidating, she was nothing compared to her husband, Mr. Miller. They met on his vacation in China twenty years ago, and he brought her back to his hometown in Ohio for marriage. They moved to the Austin area when they decided to start a family. However, for some reason, she didn't change her last name.

Jin entered the house, and Mrs. Zhao led him to the dining room where Ethan was eating some scrambled eggs, potatoes, and sautéed peppers. His tall frame and broad shoulders made the plate of food in front of him look tiny. When Ethan noticed Jin walking in, he made a grin so large that it should not have been able to fit on his small face.

"Oh my, is really that Seokjin Yi? Oh, Sleeping Beauty, you look stunning today."

"Binyuan, no need to tease," Mrs. Zhao said, swatting her son's head. She was the only one who called Ethan by his Chinese name, probably because she was the one who gave it to him. "Hold tight, Jin. I'll get you a plate too."

"Thank you, ma'am."

"Why'd you go last night? You left right when it was getting fun," Ethan said slowly, being careful not to reveal that they were at a club to his mom. "I bet you just left to play VMA huh?"

Jin pulled back a chair and took a seat. "How'd you know?"

"My third eye sees everything. It knows everything. It sees into your soul."

"Does your third eye know I think you have a nice ass?"

Laughter erupted out of Ethan's mouth, sounding like the screech of some sort of aquatic animal pleading for help. Jin couldn't hold his laughter, either. Ethan's laughing was way funnier than the joke itself.

"Calm down," Mrs. Zhao said. She walked to the table and placed some food, utensils, and a glass of water in front of Jin. "Oh yeah, Binyuan, I forgot to tell you this morning. Jared is coming home soon."

Ethan's eyes widened. "Wait what? Really? Why?"

"I think he has some sort of conference in the area. He said he'd pay us a quick visit!"

"Oh no," Ethan said, leaning back and covering his face with his hands.

Jared was Ethan's older brother. He was in his midtwenties and grew up to be the pinnacle of success. Apparently, when he was seventeen like Jin and Ethan, he was at the top of his class, was a nationally ranked lacrosse player, and a genius pianist. When he graduated, he worked as an engineer in the Silicon Valley before creating his own start-up which gathered millions from investors. He was the type of child that parents like the Millers could never stop bragging about.

Honestly, Jin thought Ethan was on the same track to becoming just as successful as a top student and VR Fighter, but for some reason, he hated his brother. He didn't want to be associated with him.

The conversation had stopped until Mrs. Zhao sat at the table to eat with them. "By the way, Jin, congratulations on qualifying for nationals!"

Jin smiled. "It was all luck. I haven't even been doing well. I only got in because of a single decent result a few months ago."

Athletes could qualify for nationals either by being ranked in the top twenty in their region or by having individually impressive results. This was usually determined by a regional representative of the VR Association. Something about that tournament impressed somebody, but Jin had no idea why. Ethan qualified by his firm twelfth seat in Texas.

Mrs. Zhao shrugged. "Well you're going now, and that's all that matters. I'm happy for you."

Jin smiled back. "Thank you."

"When is the competition again?" She asked.

"The first weekend of July," Ethan said before Jin could react. "I don't remember the exact date, though."

"Oh that's good to hear," she said, sipping her water. "I was worried it was going to interfere with school."

Ethan shook his head. It was currently April—about a month left of school and a few months before the tournament.

Suddenly, the front door opened. Mrs. Zhao turned. "Oh honey, what brings you home so early?"

Jin's heart dropped. It was Mr. Miller.

"Oh, not much," Mr. Miller said with a sigh. "I just realized I should probably fetch some of the old prototypes I left in the garage."

Mr. Miller was an engineer. Jin wasn't really sure what type, but he knew that he worked closely with the government, in the most prestigious collective of engineers in the state. They were looked up to, but they were also worked to the bone.

Jin could feel his presence walking toward the dining table. He could hear his footsteps get louder and louder with every step. However, Jin could not bring himself to look at him.

"What is this boy doing here again?" Mr. Miller's voice boomed, almost as if it were echoing.

Mrs. Zhao looked up, flustered. "Oh, well I just thought it'd be okay to have him over for breakfast for a bit…"

"We've had this conversation before. This child has no life, no future. He doesn't even go to school. How could you let such a thug be around our children?"

Silence. Jin could feel his legs quiver. He was terrified.

"Dad," Ethan said. "It's not Jin's fault that he doesn't go to school."

His father slowly took off his jacket and placed it on the coat hanger.

"Then whose fault is it? His dead mother's?"

No response. From the corner of his eye, Jin could see Ethan clenching his jaw, but he didn't mind. Ethan always took attacks against Jin worse than Jin himself took them. However, he was surprised. He couldn't remember the last time Ethan talked back to his father. The very idea frightened Jin to his core.

Mr. Miller walked to the dining table, every step squeezing Jin's heart tighter and tighter. Jin kept his head locked downward, looking at the floor. He knew Mr. Miller was beside him when he could see his feet.

"Get out of this house." The words felt heavy, as if they were spoken with violent intent.

Jin finally turned to face the father of the house. The man's tall, dark stature seemed to kiss the ceiling. His button-up shirt and trousers were flawlessly tailored to his massive body, and his face seemingly naturally aged into the shape of a deep frown. He gazed downward with a disgusted expression on his face, as if he was looking at an insect.

"I want you to get out—*now*," he repeated.

Jin simply nodded, stood up, and left. Nobody escorted him out.

Before Jin could even leave the front lawn, he got a notification on his phone. It was a text from Ethan.

"Sorry about that, man. I really didn't know my dad would be coming home. To say sorry, let me take you somewhere tonight. Be ready to be picked up at 8:00 p.m."

John didn't respond—he wasn't really in the mood. He just walked back to his house, with his mind not really focused on anything.

CHAPTER 3

Jin patiently stood among the shoppers of the dingy electronics shop, waiting for his tournament results to appear on the monitor. He already knew where he would be: sixteenth place—a mediocre result considering there were only thirty competitors. However, waiting for the official release was second nature to him now, a habit made back when he was excited to see how he'd done.

It was just a local competition held in an old store in Bezo every other Saturday, nothing serious. Attendance was never quite spectacular, but the event was particularly empty that night. Not even Ethan came. However, Jin couldn't imagine doing anything else with his time. VMA was his life.

When the results were finally displayed, he headed straight for the exit. There was hardly any reaction; he'd done this dozens of times before.

Outside, the indiscernible sounds of chatting pedestrians, zooming cars, and street performers blended into a pleasant white noise. It wasn't quite like downtown, but he still enjoyed it, especially now that the sun had gone down.

He was barely out the door before he was interrupted.

"Hey, you," a voice called.

He turned to see a girl around his age standing by the doorway. She had short blond hair that came to her shoulders, and her hands were buried in the pockets of a sleek leather jacket. However, her skirt, handbag, and black army boots made her look girly.

Jin stared. He was unsure whether she was addressing him or someone else.

"Yeah, you. I need to ask you a question," she continued, audibly annoyed by his confusion.

Shit.

Suddenly, she moved in uncomfortably close. The two were nearly face-to-face, and Jin could clearly smell her flowery perfume. He took a half-step back out of instinct.

"Your name is Seokjin, right?" She spoke with a sharp, confident cadence, as if she were sure she already knew the answer.

"Um, yes."

"Good, 'cause I'm curious." She leaned forward and looked into his eyes. "Why do you keep competing when you're not good?"

Jin froze. It wasn't that rare for him to get aggressive comments, but he was still caught off guard by how abruptly this came.

"I just…" He couldn't finish his sentence. His brain felt empty.

She sighed. "All right sorry, no offense. I just want to know. What exactly do you have to gain from this? It doesn't make sense to me."

He tried to come up with the right words to respond with, but he couldn't find them. He could feel his face getting flushed. Now she was silent, waiting for his response. Her face was calm, but her piercing gaze had an agonizing intensity.

"It's because it's what I'm meant to do." The words finally burst out of Jin's mouth. "Plus, I owe someone."

The girl blinked for a moment as if she were startled, but her face remained expressionless.

"Hey, hey, isn't that Jin?" a voice shouted.

A few feet away, Liam Kuldell and two friends were walking down the street toward them. Jin could instantly recognize Liam's tall, slim figure and dirty blond hair.

"Hey yeah, I was right. It's him," Liam said, grinning. "How've you been man?"

Liam's tone was oddly friendly. He was probably in a good mood. Everyone in the VR community knew Liam. It wasn't that he was a particularly great athlete, but his ego wouldn't let him enter a room without making sure everybody knew he was there. He also had a reputation for getting violent. Some seemed to be attracted to this. Liam could always be seen goofing off with a group of his goons. Those who joined his clique eventually came to mimic Liam. They dressed in similar trendy clothing, got similar wavy hairstyles, and vaped e-cigarettes constantly. However, no matter how hard they tried, none of them could replicate Liam's precise presence.

"Oh hey," Jin replied. For the first time ever, he felt a bit relieved to see Liam. He couldn't be that much worse than the girl beside him.

"Man, I heard you qualified for nationals," Liam said, chuckling. "I'm impressed."

Jin let out a fake laugh. "Thanks."

"I guess I'll see you there then. I qualified the same way you did. I've been playing pretty well lately."

"Congrats, man." Jin wanted to be friendly, but he didn't really know what else to say.

"Oh wait, how could I forget?" Liam dragged out the friends beside him. "These are my friends, Lucas and Collin."

Lucas was a lanky kid with buzz cut, and Collin was a shorter boy with a thick neck. Jin could tell right away that they were new to Liam's group. He greeted them both and shook their hands.

Liam poked his head out between his two lackey's shoulders. "Well, now that I've introduced my friends, you have to introduce yours now. Who's the girl?"

Jin turned around. The aggressive girl was still there. He hadn't even noticed. Unlike before, she was silent the entire time.

She stepped forward. "My name is Charlotte."

Liam smiled. Jin could tell from his eyes that he was looking her up and down, checking her out. "Man, I think this has got to be the first time I've ever seen you with a girl. What a bizarre sight. I don't think I've ever even seen you talk to a girl before. I didn't know you had those kind of balls."

The three friends started laughing. Charlotte didn't seem to find it funny. She stayed put with the same expressionless, blank stare.

"So, Jin, what school do you go to?" Lucas asked.

He paused. Liam smiled and wiped his forehead, as if to say "he doesn't know yet."

"I…don't go to school," Jin said.

Silence.

"Oh," Lucas said with a small smile. "Do you work?"

Liam reeled back to hide his snickering.

"No, I don't. I'm just…doing VMA."

More silence.

Collin crinkled up his nose. "Well, why the fuck are you doing that?"

Liam's laughter finally burst out of his mouth. Collin turned. "What man? Weren't you thinking the same thing?"

"I was, I was," Liam cackled, putting his hand on Collin's shoulder. "I really taught you how to grow a pair, huh? I'm proud."

Collin smirked and turned back to Jin. "Listen, if you don't go to school, then what the hell are you gonna do instead? You know how competitive it is when you get older. Are you not thinking about the future?"

Jin didn't have a good answer to this question.

Lucas leaned forward, playing off Collin's rudeness. "Actually, now that we mention it, aren't you the guy who's always following Ethan around? What the fuck is a nobody doing around someone who actually has respect?"

Jin didn't have an answer to that either. Perhaps it was just Ethan's kindness. Or maybe Ethan hung out with him out of pity. He wasn't sure, but he knew the boys weren't expecting an actual answer.

"Look who the fuck is talking." Charlotte stomped toward the boys. Her face was no longer calm—there was anger drawn all over it. "Why the fuck is a nobody like you following around somebody like Liam?"

Lucas flinched and his face grew as red as a tomato.

"And you." Charlotte faced Collin with her arms folded. "If you're thinking about the future so much, then why are you spending your time hanging around with a fucker like Liam? I mean, yeah, I guess living in someone's shadow as their lackey would be an amazing way develop respect and a promising life huh?"

Collin's mouth was wide open. He looked as if he were trying to find the words to say, but they weren't there.

Liam stepped forward, this time with a deathly serious look on his face. "All right, that's enough."

Charlotte snorted. "Yeah? The fuck are you gonna do?" She leaned back with a grin. She looked like she was about to chuckle. Liam must have been more than a foot taller than her, but she was glaring up straight into his eyes.

He clenched his jaw. His veins were almost visibly popping out of his forehead. "This bitch…" He muttered, raising his arm.

Suddenly, Charlotte whipped out a canister of pepper spray from her handbag and blasted Liam's face. Before Jin could react, she grabbed his hand and fled the other direction.

She dragged him through the pedestrians littering the streets. Jin could hear Liam groaning in pain behind them. When he turned around, he could see the three chasing them. Liam's face was red with rage and dripping with tears and sweat.

At the end of the street, Charlotte turned the corner and led Jin to a metal staircase behind a tall building. The staircase trembled as the two dashed up it. The angry boys' voices followed close behind.

When they reached the top, they found themselves on the roof. Charlotte let go of Jin's hand. "Follow my lead." She began sprinting toward the other side. Then she jumped, lifting off, through the air, and onto the roof of the building next door.

He froze. *Did she really just do that?*

Jin could hear the boys getting close. He didn't have any time to think. He followed her and bolted, launching off the ledge and trying not to look down.

As soon as his foot made contact with the neighboring building, he slipped. He dropped stomach-first onto the rim of the roof. Charlotte grabbed him by the elbows and jerked him up.

"QUICK. NOW." She lifted him up and threw him behind a generator. She dove next to him. They flattened themselves on the ground just as Liam and his gang reached the adjacent roof.

"FUCK, WHERE ARE THEY?" Liam's voice boomed in frustration.

The two didn't need to exchange any words to know they had to be absolutely quiet. However, Jin couldn't control his panting. His lungs burned. He tried to keep as silent as possible, but he wasn't sure if it was too loud.

The two hid until they were sure the boys had left.

"What the fuck was that?" Jin asked, sitting up and gasping for air. Everything had happened so fast that he began to feel dizzy.

Charlotte turned, starting to catch her breath as well. "That was fun!"

He rolled over with a dumbfounded look on his face.

Charlotte smirked. "I've lived in this area for a long time. I know all the shortcuts and buildings that are jumpable."

In that moment, Jin felt many things, too many to count, but he didn't have the energy to talk back.

"Look, Jin. I'm sorry for talking to you like that when we first met." Charlotte looked up at the sky. "I realized that probably wasn't too different from how those guys just talked to you."

He closed his eyes. He was surprised she had apologized. He couldn't remember the last time somebody apologized to him for being rude. He tried to calm down and gather his breath a bit before responding.

"It's okay, Charlotte. Thank you."

She looked over and smiled. "Call me Char. That's what important people call me."

CHAPTER 4

Jin's near-death experience last night was nothing but an amusing story to Ethan over the phone.

"So you're telling me that a girl pepper sprayed Liam and made you jump off a building with her?" Ethan chuckled. "Did you at least get her name?"

He hesitated as he tried to remember. "She said her name was Charlotte. She goes by Char though."

Ethan hollered. "Jesus man, now this is finally making sense. She goes to my school. Everyone knows her. She's like a local celebrity."

"For?"

"Well, she's…" Ethan paused. "Let's just say she's weird. People think she's a sociopath."

"What?"

"Like, she doesn't have any empathy for other human beings. She's really smart, ranked second in our class, and she's even rich. But she doesn't really have friends because she's rude to basically everyone, probably 'cause she doesn't find anyone deserving of her respect."

"I see." He had an idea of what Ethan was talking about.

"Girls don't approach her 'cause she has a foul mouth, and boys don't approach her 'cause she's too intimidating. She usually just minds her own business, doing her own thing, but every now and then, she does something crazy that everyone at school talks about for the next week. This might become one of those crazy things."

"It won't if you don't tell anyone."

Ethan laughed. "We'll see. Anyway, I have to go. Got errands to run for my family. Let me know if you ever run into Charlotte again."

He hung up.

Jin was left alone, lying on his bed and staring at the ceiling. The frantic yelling from last night was fresh in his ears. He could still practically feel the tension in his legs as they had jumped from the roof. And now, everything felt so eerily silent in comparison.

He began to think about the future. Maybe Liam's friends had a point.

The dark crevices of his room began to slither through the shadows. *What are you going to do with no education, no achievements, and no success?*

He felt petrified—paranoid of the space around him. He felt his lungs were being stripped of air, no, he felt like he was drowning. It was inevitable. There would be nowhere else to run, not even his own room. He clutched his heart; he could feel it beating erratically.

Suddenly, a text from Coach Arby.

Hey Jin! Wanna eat lunch by the river today?

He sat up and gasped for air. The text pulled him back to reality. This often happened whenever he was alone for too long. No matter how long he avoided them, those thoughts always came back. He knew he'd have to confront them eventually, but he couldn't imagine doing so anytime soon. He knew avoiding them was only a temporary fix to a bigger issue, but he didn't know what else to do.

Once he got a grip of himself, he dragged himself to the bathroom to wash up and brush his teeth before responding to Arby.

* * *

When Jin arrived, he saw Arby sitting on a picnic blanket spread out on the ground beside the river. In one hand, he was reading a book, and in the other was a sandwich that he snuck bites from. Beside him was a small camping cooler and a stack of books, many of which didn't seem to have covers. The soft humming of his usual wireless portable kettle and gentle flowing of the river was white noise to the silence of the field.

"Hey Arby," Jin called out.

The coach didn't react, his body remaining as still as a statue aside from his chewing.

"ARBY."

He jumped a bit and looked up.

"SHIT." Arby put his book down. "Don't startle me like that, I'm getting too old."

"Sorry."

"Whatever, take a seat. I've got the food right here." Arby slapped the cooler beside him. "I'm boiling the water for tea too. You want some?"

"Yeah." Jin opened the cooler and saw a row of tidy sandwiches, organized by fillings. There must have been at least a dozen of them originally, but Arby had probably eaten most of them. Jin always thought it was funny how cleanly he liked to organize food before devouring all of it in an instant.

He grabbed a sandwich and sat next to Arby. "I got in a fight yesterday."

Arby leaned forward. "Oh?"

"The usual. Although this time it escalated 'cause of a girl."

Arby turned away and nodded. He was the only one who Jin felt comfortable talking about this with. He was the only other bum who sympathized with him. Arby's silent nod spoke far more to Jin than the fake words of others.

"You know, back in the day, it wasn't all that uncommon for people to not go to school," Arby said.

Jin raised his brows. "Really?"

Arby nodded. "Well, I suppose it was still rare for people to not even go to middle school like you…but there were a fair number who stopped around high school. I would say it certainly wasn't unheard of."

Jin plopped his chin into his palm and stared at Arby, as if to ask, "What happened?"

Arby looked up at the clouds. "The world changed. You have to be really good at what you do to lead a decent life these days."

"Did you not need to before?"

Arby paused. "It was the machines. We used to do all the jobs they did. Driving. Cooking. Farming. Almost every career that a robot can do has been taken over. It only gets worse and worse. Now, everyone wants to either learn to do something that machines can't do or learn how to make the machines. We lost a lot of jobs, and people have to go to school now to get whatever's available."

Jin nodded. He'd heard stuff like this before, but he hadn't really thought about it very much.

"It got competitive. Real competitive," Arby continued. "So much so that they even got machines to hire people too. They developed the Career Algorithm when demand for it rose among companies hiring."

The Career Algorithm. A name that loomed over the minds of Jin's entire generation. It was a system that took all information about a person—their background, race, grades, location, and basically anything else that was legally obtainable—and compiled it into a score from one to one thousand. This score would indicate how fit the applicant was for the position; all employers had to do was choose the highest score.

"At first, people were against the idea of an algorithm controlling so much. They didn't want to reduce people to just a number. In fact, many are still against it because it proliferates systemic injustices and all that stuff people argue about it politics… But it's still used by every big corporation. It's too convenient not to."

"So did you used to work a job that machines took?" Jin asked.

Arby shook his head. "No, I've always been in sports. Although, I did work as a waiter at some point."

The two didn't speak for a moment. Suddenly, the kettle clicked. The water was done boiling. Jin hadn't been paying attention to it, but the kettle was rather loud at this point. Arby grabbed it and poured the water into two cups with tea bags. He placed one on the ground in front of Jin.

The two sipped in silence.

"I chose this life, though," Arby said, putting down his drink. "I used to have a family, but when things didn't work out, I was the one who wanted to be a nomad. I was the one who wanted to ignore society."

Jin nearly choked on the scalding tea. "Wait, you had a family? Where are they now?"

Arby took a deep breath out of his nose, facing the river. "Who knows."

Silence again. Now, the two were looking back at the river, flowing toward wherever the current took it.

"You're young, though. You still have your whole life ahead of you."

Jin shrugged.

Arby took another sip. "You're different from me. I know you didn't choose this life."

Jin turned quickly. That caught him off guard. However, he just turned back toward the river and remained silent. He didn't know how to feel. Arby was right, though; he wasn't satisfied. He'd dropped everything to chase VR Fighting, and he hated himself for doing so. But despite this, the emotions from back then were still crystal clear. He'd had no other choice.

"Arby," he said.

"Hmm?"

"What do you think it takes to live a good life?"

Arby shifted in his seat and uncrossed his legs. The still look on his face was indecipherable. Jin wasn't expecting a specific answer. He was sure Arby was still mulling over this type of thing for himself.

Arby finished his tea before finally responding. "You know what they used to think about when trying to answer that question? Have you ever heard of Sisyphus?"

Jin shook his head.

"He's a figure in Greek mythology who was punished by the gods for cheating death. When they found out, they punished him by making him roll a boulder up a hill. Whenever he would reach the top, the boulder would roll back down the hill, and he would have to start over. He would be stuck doing this for all eternity, just rolling up that rock and seeing it fall back down."

The feeling felt a little too close for comfort for Jin.

Arby continued. "Here's what all those old philosophers were thinking about: is there any meaning to Sisyphus' existence?"

"I guess it doesn't seem so."

"So here's where that conversation leads to—why? Why exactly doesn't it have meaning? It seems intuitive that this life is meaningless, but what specifically about eternally rolling that rock is so meaningless? Is it because he does the same thing over and over and over again? Is it because rolling that rock doesn't make any meaningful difference? Is it because the life would be miserable? See, if one can pinpoint exactly what makes something meaningless, then that would be a key to understanding what it means for a life to be meaningless."

Jin sat still, staring at the sky and the boulder-shaped clouds. "I think I'm following."

Arby started to smile and bounce as he spoke. He always got excited when he talked about this kind of thing. Jin enjoyed letting him go and seeing where his thoughts took them.

"To pinpoint exactly why Sisyphus' life was so pointless, philosophers asked more questions. What if Sisyphus actually loved pushing that rock up the hill? What if it was his life's passion, and he could never grow sick of rock pushing? Or what if pushing that rock actually caused some sort of net good onto society? Like every time he reached the top of the hill, someone in the world would be cured of their illnesses? Once we think of these examples, it wouldn't be too much further of a reach to swap them out. Instead of Sisyphus loving to push that rock forever, maybe he enjoys playing games or singing forever. And instead of curing someone every time he reached the top, he was stuck doing charity work or being a doctor his whole life."

Arby was leaning forward now and talking animatedly with his hands. He was clearly really enjoying this. Jin smiled.

"I would imagine that there's some subjectivity to this, then. It would depend on how you define 'meaningful,'" Jin said. He'd talked with Arby enough to be able to catch on to this kind of thing.

"Yes! Exactly!" Arby said, raising his hands and smiling. "Many philosophers ultimately came to their own conclusions on the nature of 'meaning.' Of course, all of them have a line of reasoning that are, to various degrees, justified. However, when you ask what makes a life meaningless, you also have to ask, what does meaningless even mean?"

Jin snickered and nodded. His tea had gotten cold now, but he drank the rest anyway. "And so, I would imagine, for many people, leading a meaningful life isn't exactly the same as a life that you're satisfied with."

Arby's eyes lit up. "Exactly!" Jin knew exactly how to incite Arby's passion. "So if a meaningful life, whatever it may be, and a satisfied life are likely two different things, then what's even the value of a meaningful life? Why would I want a meaningful life? Why would I want it over one I found fulfilling?"

Jin nodded, thinking about the "meaning" as they'd discussed it. Suddenly, Arby squirmed and slouched over.

"Sorry if I got carried away again."

Jin laughed. "No, no, you know I enjoy it."

Arby still seemed embarrassed.

The two continued to stare at the river. It shone with the reflection of the sunlight and gently hummed. The water's clear, perpetual movement was hypnotizing. However, despite having seen this river hundreds of times now, there was something about the flowing water that captured Jin today.

CHAPTER 5

The news exploded overnight. By Saturday morning, there wasn't a single VR Fighter in the Austin area that didn't know—Magnus had registered in a local fight.

Magnus Andersen was a god among fighters. At only fourteen years old, he was already competing at the national level, and now, at sixteen, he was one of the best in the world. He was a rising star in the US, giving hope that the nation's next generation of fighters had a good footing on the international stage. He was a big deal, and it was sometimes strange to think that such a high-profile competitor was living right here in the area.

However, he had practically never competed within the state. It was below him. He didn't need to compete at regionals to qualify for national or international events given his ranking, so he didn't waste his time.

But this competition was an anomaly. He'd registered for this relatively average regional competition, probably just to get in a bit of low-level practice before nationals.

When Jin saw Magnus on the tournament's list of competitors, he couldn't believe his eyes. He immediately dropped out. He couldn't even think about playing in the same hall as

Magnus. Ethan hadn't registered either, but that was because it was almost the end of April, and school was approaching its final stretch. They hadn't been friends with Magnus since the incident, and Jin couldn't see himself confronting him now.

Yet, to his own surprise, he still found himself waking up and going to the tournament that morning. His body moved on its own, as if watching Magnus fight was a given.

The tournament venue was located downtown, and the interior had beige, patterned walls with brown carpet. It felt more like a hotel than the hub of a gaming tournament to Jin. The entire event was essentially held in one large hall with VR stations scattered throughout. Clearly a low-budget competition. Jin hated events like these, where players and spectators were expected to just wander around in the same, cluttered hall.

When Jin arrived, there was still an hour or so before competitors were required to check in. Only a handful of players were in the hall warming up. He found an empty wall to lean against with a clear view of the entrance. As more people trickled in, he grew restless. He stopped looking away at his phone or at other players warming up and kept a laser focus on the door.

Suddenly, there he was. Magnus walked through the door wearing a techy, black sports hoodie, track pants, and a gray backpack. It wasn't just Jin that noticed him—everyone in the hall seemed to hold their breath. He was tall, hovering over even the relatively tall players in the room. His hands were stuffed in his pockets, and he walked with a relaxed, mature demeanor. He stood out; it was hard to believe he was just a high schooler.

Numerous eyes followed him as he strutted through the venue. He seemed unfazed, however, and casually plopped his bag next to a VR station and got ready to hook up. Slowly, a mob of fans started to form around the station, hoping to see his warm-up routine on the station's monitor.

Jin stayed put. He was tempted to join the crowd, but he was scared Magnus would spot him. He stood still against the wall, just observing. After a while, his muscles started to stiffen up, but his body wouldn't dare move an inch.

When the competition finally began, players moved to their assigned stations for the first round. It was obvious which station was Magnus' based off the circle of spectators hovering around him. Jin finally moved when some time had passed and he was certain Magnus wouldn't catch sight of him. He crept across the room and stood behind the crowd to watch Magnus.

Jin was startled at what he saw. After only about ten minutes, the match was already coming to a close, 48–10. Magnus only needed one good combination to end this.

But it was apparent that Magnus was in no rush to finish. He was hopping on his toes, bouncing in and out of distance, juggling his iron bar without actually making any attacks. He already knew he was going to win.

It was unlikely any spectator disagreed. The difference in level was clear. Even Magnus' bouncing had an elegance to it.

When Magnus seemed bored enough, he shifted gears, suddenly bending his knees before shifting his weight into a swift whack against his opponent's head. He won.

When the two unplugged from the VR station, Magnus' opponent reached out to shake his hand. This guy didn't seem bothered by the loss at all, a rare occurrence in the VMA tournaments.

The match ended before most others were even halfway done. In addition, not even two points of damage had been taken from Magnus' health score. All his matches that day were the same way. They were some of the most peaceful fights Jin had ever witnessed. Magnus' movements just felt so effortless, requiring the bare minimum focus to replay the drills ingrained into his muscle memory.

Most of his opponents barely raised their intensity as well. They knew they couldn't win anyway. Some would occasionally put in more effort, seemingly to test their limits, but Magnus didn't even seem to notice. To him, players of this level putting in a full hundred percent or just twenty percent effort was exactly the same.

Before Jin knew it, the tournament had already arrived at the gold medal match, and half the day had gone by. All of Magnus' matches seemed so similar that they had blended together.

His final opponent was Luke Seeger. A respectable player. He might've even had a chance to get more than ten points off Magnus.

There was a large break between the semifinals and gold medal match. Organizers usually did this for the final match to build suspense, but there wasn't any to speak of. Everyone knew who was going to win. If anything, the break was a source of aggravation, leaving Jin and every other spectator waiting in front of the VR station. He grew impatient; his knees were starting to hurt from standing all day.

"Jin!" A voice suddenly said beside him.

He turned his head and saw Char squeezing herself through the crowd to reach him. He was caught off guard— he hadn't seen her in a week.

"I knew you'd be here," she said, securing a spot next to him. "I just needed to pick you apart from the crowd."

"Why are you here?"

"I heard this was an interesting tournament," Char said, swaying her hips.

"Well, it's definitely special. Magnus is here. It's not exactly interesting though. He's basically just been kicking everyone's ass."

She chuckled.

Before they could speak any further, the two players had hooked up to their stations and the match began. The crowd around the station tightened as spectators squeezed closer to watch.

As the countdown started, Magnus bent his knees and readied his stance. He took a deep breath. He was about to fight seriously.

Luke did the same. He chose the spear as his weapon.

Three, two, one… GO!

Magnus lunged toward Luke.

Luke raised his spear.

Magnus swung his bar around the spear with swift precision, as if he'd already seen it coming.

Smack.

The first hit. And then another one. And then a swipe with the elbow. And a knee. Magnus was completely capitalizing on the combination. Luke couldn't keep up. His comparatively sluggish movements made it look almost unfair.

Magnus didn't stop. He just kept hitting, and hitting, and hitting, driving his opponent into the corner.

Soon, Luke's back actually hit the virtual wall surrounding the stage. Magnus didn't slow down. There was no room for Luke to move at all.

And just like that, without warning, Luke's health bar reached zero. Magnus had won 50–0.

The crowd was speechless. No mercy was shown. The match was just Magnus smacking Luke mercilessly for a minute straight.

Char was the first one to break the silence. "Wow."

When the two unplugged, they shook hands. Despite being completely embarrassed in front of such a big crowd of people, Luke didn't seem to mind.

Magnus shook his hand but didn't seem interested. He went through the motions quickly, and yanked his hand away as soon as was socially acceptable. However, when he turned to walk off, he paused for a moment and looked at the crowd. Jin could feel it. They made eye contact.

Then, Magnus walked off, snatching his bag and heading for the door. Slowly, the crowd started to die down, but Jin stayed put. He started to feel a shiver down his spine, for some reason feeling a delayed reaction from Magnus' glare.

"Hey, hey." Char nudged, cutting through the silence. "Jin, I'm curious."

"Yeah?" he responded, snapping back to reality.

"How do the rules actually work in this sport?"

He turned his head. "Wait, you don't know how to play?"

Char shrugged. "Well, I think I get the basics. You just hit them until you win."

Jin was astonished. "Why are you always watching it then?"

She paused, eyes bouncing between Jin and the space behind him. "Not sure."

Jin didn't know what to say.

"Well, maybe you could teach me some time," she said. "It'd be cool to actually know what's going on in y'all's heads."

He agreed, not knowing what he was getting himself into.

* * *

When Jin returned home, he saw his dad at home—for the first time in weeks. He was startled to see his father. Mr. Ewhan Yi worked for the police, but Jin wasn't exactly sure what kind of work he did. He never really wanted to ask. The only thing he knew was that his father held some sort of powerful position, and that he could set his own hours. Ever since his wife died, he'd practically lived in his office. Jin honestly wasn't even sure if his father came home most days.

But here he was, sitting in silence at the dining table. His thin, black hair was parted to the side, and he was still dressed in a uniform: a black button-up shirt with pockets and badges scattered across the fabric. There was an opened bottle of beer before him on the table, but it seemed to be completely full.

Mr. Yi didn't drink. Jin's guess was that he'd tried just now but couldn't get himself to follow through.

Jin stood in front of his father for what seemed like a few minutes before he finally noticed his son's presence.

"Oh, you're home, Jin!" Mr. Yi said with a wide, kind smile. He was a passive man who always seemed to be smiling despite his tired, baggy eyes. The last time Jin could remember being yelled at by his father was when he was a child.

His father's smile annoyed Jin. It just seemed so artificial, as if he was putting on a show for others.

"Yeah, I'm home."

"How was your day?"

Jin paused. His father hadn't asked him about his day in a long time.

"It was good."

Mr. Yi smiled again. "Good."

There was a stillness, as if both parties were expecting the other to do something. However, looking at his father irked Jin. He pitied his father—a man who had not been able to cope with the loss of his wife, now stuck in a self-torturous cycle of work. However, Jin couldn't stand to think about it. It confronted him with just how much of a hypocrite he was himself.

And without saying a word, Jin left the dining room to go to his room. The conversation had ended.

CHAPTER 6

For the first time in years, the smooth, waxy leather stuck out to Jin as he crushed it with his knuckles. It was just him and Arby, going through drills with the boxing mitts on a Saturday morning as usual. Jin had trained those sequences for as long as he could remember; it was his usual routine. But today was different. July seventeenth—exactly one week before nationals.

It was a strange feeling. He could perform the familiar drills as mindlessly as usual, but minor, trivial things stuck out. The thump of his arms as he struck, the bouncing of his hair as he moved, and the friction of his toes in his virtual shoes. They were things he'd never really thought about before but couldn't help but noticing today.

He'd always been like this, always prone to distraction. He hated this about himself. His mind just loved wandering, usually at precisely the wrong time. Perhaps it was because of the adhd that his doctor wouldn't diagnose him with. Or perhaps he was afraid of putting in his complete, undivided attention only to fail. Or maybe it was his inability to follow through with his passions. Or maybe he was just dumb.

He hated it. He absolutely hated it. It made him feel like he had no control. If he couldn't even control his own head, how could he have any control over his own life? Given his life so far, the evidence seemed to support this noncontrol conclusion, but it was something that he wouldn't accept. Even if it was what he actually believed on the inside.

thump. thump.

Jin started to hit harder. Was it frustration? No. Perhaps denial. But how could he be in denial when he recognized it as denial?

Regardless, he was stuck. He didn't know what else awaited him besides nationals. It was all he had.

smack.

He finished and took a breather. *How did this happen?*

He knew why. It was because of VMA.

He chose this sport in middle school. It was his thirteenth birthday—and there was no way in hell that Jin was going to go to math tutoring. Such an event marked his transition to a teenager, something middle schoolers only experience once. He wanted that day to be special; what he really wanted to do was try VR Fighting even just once. His parents were against it—they said it was too violent for a kid his age. But how could he possibly do math that day when there was such a good opportunity to do something cooler? His parents made him go to tutoring every single Friday, so how much harm could missing one day really cause?

Once the bell rang and class was dismissed, Jin got a notification on his phone. He already knew his mom would be parked by the front entrance, waiting to ruin his birthday with math. But luckily, he knew just the person to help him escape.

He ran down the hall to Ethan's classroom. Most of the kids in his class were on their way out, but Ethan had still not taken a step away from his seat. When he entered the room, Ethan turned and grinned.

"I've been waiting for you, young grasshopper," Ethan said.

"Wipe that smile off your face, you look stupid," Jin said. "You know what we have to do, right?"

"I'm two, no, three steps ahead of you. I know just the place," Ethan said, still smiling.

Ethan led Jin downstairs, and when nobody else seemed to be looking, they slid into the art room. Mr. Crosley, their art teacher, always went home early because he didn't have a class during the school's last class period, so the room's lights were off and chairs put away. The two friends dodged some canvases to reach the window overlooking the field and playground behind the school. They quietly slid it open and jumped out, reaching the back fence, where a small hole dug through the dirt beneath was waiting for them. They threw their backpacks over the fence and crawled through the hole to freedom.

When they reached the other side, Jin got another notification on his phone, but this time he opened his messenger.

Mom:
I've arrived. - 3:01 p.m.
Where are you? - 3:12 p.m.

He couldn't think of a response that wouldn't get him busted, so he decided to respond later.

The two boys walked a few blocks down to the playground of the old elementary school before it was moved closer to the city. This had always been their meeting spot. This was the school that Jin, Ethan, and their friends Henry and Sebastian went to before splitting their separate ways to go to different middle schools. The playground was filled with colorful slabs that had dulled with age. They were stacked on top of each other in various arrangements to create staircases, platforms, and mazes that contained many, many memories for the friends.

Underneath a tall tower that led up to a slide, Henry and Sebastian were waiting. Henry was a short kid who apparently spent an hour every morning doing his hair in a quaff and choosing his outfit, and Sebastian was a timid kid whose family apparently had a lot of money.

"What took y'all so long?" Henry asked.

Ethan smacked his back. "Come on man, you know y'all's school is closer than ours."

Henry slapped him back.

Sebastian stood up and stretched. "So what are we doing for Jin's birthday? Didn't you say you had something prepared, Ethan?"

Ethan stopped slapping Henry for a moment and turned. "Oh yeah. You guys will love this." He grabbed his backpack and opened it for the friends to peer through. Inside were two small VR sets and some neatly coiled wires. Ethan turned toward Jin. "I know you've really wanted to try VR stuff, so I got my hands on some headsets. Happy birthday, man."

Jin was ecstatic. He gave Ethan a fist bump. Henry and Sebastian seemed pretty excited too.

"Is the headset going to mess up my hair if I put it on, though?" Henry said.

Ethan began setting up the headsets, but it took nearly half an hour. He was just as clueless as the rest of the boys. When he finally finished, the headsets turned on with a click.

Jin and Henry entered the VR room first. It was a bit strange that Ethan wasn't entering first when he was the one who set it up, but he insisted that somebody else go first. The room was wide, with panels of a fluorescent blue. The floor felt strangely familiar against the bottom of his feet, and the air was peculiarly thin.

Their headsets included a couple of complimentary games: a cooking simulator, sword fighting, and the free trial of a fantasy adventure game. The kids mainly stuck with sword fighting. They had absolutely no idea what was going on. They ran at each other, screaming, arms flailing, and not a care in the world.

The kids rotated through to give everyone a fair amount of playing time. Ethan won almost every game he played.

Eventually, the sun set, and the boys were about ready to do something else.

"Oh my god, why does Ethan keep winning?" Henry bemoaned.

Ethan started grinning again. "Hey, hey. I guess I really am the best here, huh. Nobody else can prove me wrong."

Jin laughed and sat down on the ground. Now that he finally had a chance to breathe, he realized just how many notifications he had on his phone. His mom had sent him a text nearly every thirty minutes.

Mom:
I've arrived. - 3:01 p.m.
Where are you? - 3:12 p.m.
Are you seeing these? - 3:30 p.m.
I went inside the school, your teacher said that you already left. - 4:00 p.m.
Jin, come on. I'm gonna leave now. - 4:30 p.m.

The concert is tonight. If you want to be a good son, at least come to that, please. - 4:58 p.m.
Just got home. Your dad can give you a ride to the concert if you come home in time. - 5:25 p.m.

Jin had forgotten about his mom's concert. She was a singer and his favorite artist.

"I'm bored of winning," Ethan said. "We already know I'm the best, why don't we find something else to do?"

Jin's eyes lit up.

"I know what we can do guys. My mom is having a concert tonight. Let's go, my dad can take us there," Jin suggested.

"A concert? Let's do something more fun," Sebastian begged.

"Hey, it's my birthday, let me call the shots tonight."

And so, the boys reluctantly left for Jin's house. Upon arrival, they found Jin's dad getting ready to leave. He always seemed to be in a good mood, but Jin noticed that he seemed particularly excited to see the kids.

"Hey! Are you guys going to the concert too?" Mr. Yi said.

The boys nodded in unison.

"Okay great, I'll get the car ready. Also, Jin, I heard you skipped tutoring and left Mom hanging. That's not nice, mister. You know how much time and money your mother and I have spent on this, right?"

Even when he was lecturing his son, Jin's dad was still smiling and speaking as if he had just cracked a joke.

"I'm sorry, Dad. I'll apologize to Mom after the concert."

"Okay, sounds good. Let's get in the car, kids!"

As everyone boarded the vehicle, Jin's friends started to giggle.

"You really got it hard, huh Jin?" Sebastian said.

Jin ignored them. In all honesty, his father didn't intimidate him, so it didn't really bother him to be lectured in front of his friends.

When they arrived at a local diner, where a corner was cleared out for the performance, Mr. Yi led the kids to a booth. They ordered food and waited for the performance to begin. When their food came, Jin's mom entered the stage from a back closet with a guitar strung around her back. She set up a microphone stand and started to tune her instrument.

When she was ready to perform, she signaled to a waiter, who signaled back an "okay."

"Hey guys," Jin's mom said. She wore a white dress and her long, dark hair fell somewhere along her back.

Most of the crowd didn't seem to notice her speaking.

"My name is Sherry Kim, I'm a singer from the area."

Most of the crowd still didn't seem to notice.

"I'm dedicating this performance to my son, who's been a bad boy today and who I know is somewhere there in the audience listening,"

All the boys at Jin's table struggled to contain their laughter.

Sherry took a deep breath and closed her eyes. She sat in silence for a moment before opening her eyes and beginning to sing in a gentle voice. Jin loved his mom's singing. It made him feel calm.

For the rest of the audience, this performance was just background music. But for Jin, it was the highlight of his day.

After the performance, Mr. Yi took all the boys home except for Jin, who wanted to hang back with his mom. He helped her pack up the performance gear, and after she picked up some cash from the restaurant's manager, she led her son to her car.

"You know, that was really rude of you to leave me hanging like that," Sherry stated.

Jin paused. "What are you talking about?"

"Oh, you know exactly what I'm talking about."

"Okay fine, I'm sorry. I just didn't really know how to get out of tutoring. It's my birthday, so I just didn't want to waste my time with stuff like math."

She sighed. "I should've seen this coming. If you really liked my singing, then you'd go to math tutoring. Where do you think all that money is coming from?"

Jin looked down and apologized again. He felt embarrassed, and he hated hearing his mom speak in that disappointed voice. His mother looked down too and paused.

"You know, I just can't stay mad at you. Not when you look so guilty like that."

Jin looked back up toward his mom.

"Here, let's go to the park. It'll help clear both of our heads. Dad won't notice."

Jin nodded and got into the car.

Sherry parked the car in front of a broad field covered with freshly mowed grass and small flowers scattered like toppings on a dessert. In the middle of the park was a pond and a small wooden shack. The two started walking on a concrete path that circled around the pond.

"What did you do today while you were out with your friends?" Sherry asked.

"I finally tried VR Fighting!" Jin said. "Ethan somehow got a VR set for us to try. It was awesome, except for the fact that Ethan kept winning."

"Ethan really is good at everything, huh?"

Jin nodded with a big smile. "He must be gifted or something."

Sherry laughed. "You're gifted too, you know."

"Really?"

"Yeah, everyone is."

Jin frowned. He'd heard stuff like that a million times.

The two moved to the grass, where they sat down, looking at the moon's reflection in the pond.

Suddenly, she got up. "Wait a second."

She walked a few feet away and carefully picked up a flower. She brought it back and showed Jin. The flower was small with dozens of luminous pink petals. "Do you know what this is called?"

He shook his head.

"It's a camellia! They're my favorite type of flower," she said, lowering her voice. "This one was picked when it was still young, and I guess somebody dropped it here. They normally grow on some sort of bush I think, and they don't have a lot of them in this part of Texas."

Jin examined the camellia carefully. He'd never seen a flower like this before.

"Do you believe in fate?" Sherry asked.

Jin shook his head. "Isn't it basically like the Career Algorithm, but what spiritual people believe in?"

"Sort of. I think fate is a bit deeper though. It goes beyond just a number," she said, looking at the pond. "I think I was fated to become a singer. I don't think that I chose that job, I think the job chose me."

Jin was confused. *How does a job choose you?* Did she just mean that she was really good at it?

She laughed, noticing the visible confusion on her son's face.

"Don't worry about it," she said. "Not everyone believes in fate, especially these days, but I do. I think fate has something good in store for you, I just know it."

"Do you think fate wants me to get into VMA?" Jin asked.

She paused. "You know, maybe. Even though your father and I said no, you still really wanted it and even found your way to VR without us."

His eyes widened. He liked where this was going.

"Can I try the real thing tomorrow?" Jin asked without thinking. The words burst out of his mouth.

She chuckled and rubbed her face. "All right, fine. You win. No matter what your dad says, I'll take you tomorrow."

Jin couldn't help but smile. He could feel himself bubbling with excitement. However, he wanted to stay mature or else his mom might change her mind. He simply relaxed down beside her and stared at the sky. He kept the camellia in his hands, not letting go until they left the park.

Looking back now, it was strange for Jin to think that this was how it all started.

CHAPTER 7

"We're here," Char said. The day had finally come for Jin to teach Char VRF. They were standing in front of a flower shop called Maria's Flowers.

It looked like any other ordinary flower shop with the same, modern glass that lined most buildings in the district. The exterior was lined with large pots housing flowers of varying lengths, a few that even crawled right out of their pot. Some were endlessly leafy, while others were nearly just a bare stalk. The petals tinted the view with yellows, purples, and orange. Jin had never seen flowers like these before—they didn't even look like they belonged on Earth.

"You live here?" Jin asked timidly, worried that he was being rude.

Char chuckled. "I live upstairs."

The two walked inside and saw racks and racks of even more exotic plants. This time, however, the gallery wasn't just limited to flowers. There were all sorts of tall ferns, leafy bushes, and fly traps that Jin had again never seen before. There was nobody in the shop except for an old woman at the cash register wearing a plain white T-shirt and a purple apron. She seemed to be staring into the air before the two entered.

"Char! Welcome back." The woman snapped back to reality with her greeting.

"Hi Maria. I've brought a friend," Char said.

Maria turned toward Jin and walked toward him. "Oh, what a fine young man you've brought," she said, reaching out to shake Jin's hand.

Jin shook it with a polite laugh. After a little more plant examining, the two left and headed toward the back exit, where an elevator was waiting for them beside a pile of boxes and plastic containers. The two got in the elevator and Char pressed the 10 button—the top floor.

"We actually didn't have to go through Maria's shop to get to the elevator. We could've just gone around the back. I just wanted you to see her stuff."

"Why's that?"

"I just thought it'd be cool. Not a lot of people seem to have an appreciation for the cool side of nature these days, so it's kind of hard to come by this sort of thing."

When the elevator opened, the two faced a hallway. Char led Jin toward room 1042, just a few doors down. Once they entered, Jin saw a tidy living room with shiny wooden flooring and a large leather couch facing windows overlooking the city. Next to this space was a kitchen and dining room with a large, marble table upon which a small vase of flowers rested.

He walked up to the windows and looked down at the people below, so small that they looked like crawling specks in the distance.

"My parents are always gone for work, but my dad put the VR stations in the guest rooms," Char said, pointing down a hall.

"You're rich enough to own a whole VR station?" Jin was impressed.

Her lips spread into a somber grin. "They have money, but it's not like it matters much. They don't care about me at all."

"I see." Jin didn't press any further. He completely related to how she felt.

She led Jin to the guest room where two stations were set neatly next to each other. Strangely, they were the only things in the room.

They sat down at a station, and soon the two were hooked up and in the VR space.

"So what exactly did you want me to do?" Jin said.

"I don't know…teach me the basics. Tell me what I'm supposed to do. I don't even know what's going on when I watch a VMA match," Char said.

"Here, I guess we can just start with the basic stance and punches," Jin said. "I'm right-handed, so I use this stance."

Jin put his left foot forward, pointed at his opponent. His fists were curled and placed right in front of his face with his elbows tucked in. Char recreated the stance without too much trouble, standing a bit awkwardly.

He extended his left hand. "This punch is called my 'one' or a jab."

He then shifted his weight and extended his right hand. "And this one is called my 'two.' We use this stance with our dominant foot back so that we can put more power into our punch when we rotate into it."

Char nodded. "Okay, so what am I supposed to do in a match? What's going on in your head when you play?"

"Hmm, I guess we can start with this." Jin walked a bit forward and held up his stance. "Right now, if we both just hold our guard, then this is a neutral position."

He moved in closer, slowly extending his arm toward Char. "If I step in and try to hit you, then I'm doing what's called 'approaching.' What do you think you'd do if you saw this?"

"Maybe step back? Or shield?"

"Yeah, those are all doable. You can also do other things like throw a counter or duck down. You can really be as creative as you want."

"I see," Char said.

"Also keep in mind, the less I commit to my attack, the quicker I can react to your defensive option and the counterattack you do after. So, for example, it's much easier for me to retreat after getting my attack shielded if it was just a short, quick jab than if I went in super close to hit you with all I've got."

Char nodded.

"So anyway, let's say I approach and you step back to make me fall short," Jin said, throwing a fake punch and deliberately missing. "Now, I'm going to keep that in mind next time I approach you. So let's say you've been able to make me miss a couple times already. This time, when I approach, I'm going to anticipate your retreat and take another step forward." He took another slow step forward and lightly tapped Char's shoulder.

She nodded her understanding and listened as Jin continued. "Now that I can predict the way you defend, I can land the hit. Same type of thinking applies when you're the one defending. If your opponent is always attacking the same way, then you'll be able to beat them once you recognize the pattern. That's why, at the most basic level, it's important to constantly mix up how you attack and defend and make your movements unpredictable."

"So is it just about who can be the most unpredictable?" Char asked.

"Well, that's definitely a big part of it. There are other types of thinking you can use too. What we just went over was taking advantage of your opponent's habits and mixing up your options so that your opponent can't do the same. You can also try to bait your opponent into doing something. Remember when I said that it's harder to react to a defensive play the more you commit to something? Well, if we can bait our opponent into committing hard to an action, then we can punish it quickly because we'll see it coming."

"What would that look like?" Char asked.

Jin thought a moment before answering. "So let's say I did a similar jab as I did before, and you shield it."

He extended another fake punch, which Char shielded. "Now, after my attack misses, I put my hands down a bit and you try to hit me back with this opening."

She swiped and he ducked under. "Like I told you before, many people will be looking to hit you in the opening that pops up when you miss an attack. That opening won't be there if we don't commit too hard to the attack, but that's not always easy to tell. So after I miss the jab, I can lower my guard to bait the attack and be ready to counter it."

Char nodded her head. "I think I'm starting to get it now, but it's a lot to wrap your head around. I didn't know fighting was actually this complicated."

"The game is all mental," Jin said. "It's not just about out-muscling your opponent, but also outthinking them."

"Question. In your example, you're letting your opponent shield your jab so that you can counter what comes next. But if you know your jab is going to be shielded in the first place, then why not just go for a shield break right off the bat? I see people use it all the time when I watch matches. Why go through these extra steps?"

"Well, you can do that against people who overuse their shield. But it's dangerous because a shieldbreaker is a move that forces you to commit really hard, so if you misjudge distance or they don't shield, then you're screwed. If you miss a jab that you didn't commit to, then you're still fine. It'll make more sense if you look at a basic strategy you can use."

Jin raised his hands into a boxing stance. "Let's say we're playing a game right now, and we're dancing in and out of attacking distance. A really simple plan I can have is to constantly harass with short jabs with the intention of having the majority of them miss. This does a couple different things. First, if I do it constantly, I can get a better feel for the distance because I can visibly see how far my punch was from hitting you. Second, I can then shift into what I was talking about before, where I sometimes jab and make it look like I committed too hard to bait a response. It would be too easy to defend if I'm just making a bunch of small jabs and then suddenly just threw out a shieldbreaker. The point is to make it all sort of blend in and, again, make yourself unpredictable. This is how you build a mind game."

Char just continued to nod. Jin wasn't quite sure if she'd retained all that information. Actually, probably not. He started to get a little embarrassed for going on a tangent.

"You really like this sport, huh?" Char asked.

Jin turned. He was caught off guard. "Why do you ask?"

"Well…people who are really drawn toward things can talk about them for a long time. It's nice hearing that passion. I can tell when they become absorbed, like they've lost track of time."

He was taken aback. He realized that he hadn't thought about his own enjoyment in a long time. He simply continued because he had to.

It was such a simple question. *Do you like VMA?*

Jin wasn't sure.

"I'm jealous of you, though," Char said.

"Huh? Why?"

"Actually, no, I hate you."

"Wait what?" Jin was spooked. He braced himself, half expecting the punchline of a joke.

"I hate that you have something you love that you can just commit your life to," she said. "I want that so badly."

He was speechless. *She doesn't understand*, he thought. It felt strange. The lifestyle he'd found himself dragged into, what he considered to be the source of most of his pain, was something she wanted.

She looked down as she continued. "It's not fair. I've been searching for something to give me purpose for so long. And people like you have had it all along. It frustrates me."

A tightness began to accumulate in Jin's heart. He hated that he never knew what to say in serious situations. "I understand," was all he could manage.

CHAPTER 8

For most of Jin's VMA career, his mom was his biggest fan. Sherry Kim didn't change her last name when she married Jin's father. She said she wanted to be her own person, so she couldn't imagine compromising something as personal as her own name. She wanted her son to carry the same energy. Her biggest fear was for him to grow into a timid person.

Perhaps that was why she grew to support her son's VMA career, even after her initial resistance. At fourteen years old, he won his first VRF tournament. It was just a regional circuit for kids in the area, but it felt like so much more. His mother definitely caught on to that.

It was a memorable competition. Once he'd reached the top eight, every match was down-to-the-wire. He couldn't remember a single match where he won by more than ten health points. He had to work for every single hit against his opponent, and he never knew he was going to win until the very last moment. After every match, Mr. Yi begged him to win by a wider margin or else he'd have a heart attack.

Back then, it felt different. Standing on the podium, receiving the gold medal, looking toward the cheering crowd—it was all a foreign feeling now.

When Jin hopped off the stage, his mom was the first to run to him. She dragged his father with her to take pictures on the new camera bought with her savings. The first pictures on it were of Jin and his father, awkwardly smiling in front of the podium with children and parents cluttered in the background.

The winning streak continued. Jin continued to place in the top three at every local and regional competition for months. He started to garner a name for himself among fighters in Bezo as a promising young talent. Word even reached Ethan's prestige-hungry parents, who eventually let their son try out the sport as well.

Once Coach Arby scouted Jin out, everything changed. Arby was a renowned coach in the state, training athletes for national and international competition. His gym was invite only, with every member handpicked by Arby himself. He kept it small to give each member the individual attention they needed to reach the top.

Jin could still remember his first day at Arby's club. His mother dropped him off. She insisted on going with him on his first day, but she eventually changed her mind when he begged her not to. She eventually succumbed, perhaps seeing how much he wanted to experience this alone.

When he opened the door, he was greeted by Coach Arby. He wore a baseball hat and slacks. Back then, that was his signature look. He began with a tour of the facility, although it wasn't much. The club was barebones, feeling almost like a stuffed warehouse. It felt serious, as if it were designed to minimize every distraction possible from VRF. He rounded off the welcoming by introducing Jin to all the members present—Arby always believed in teammates knowing each other well.

There was a tall man named Amadeus, a lanky college student named Steven, a man who had just moved from Tunisia named Fares, and many more that Jin could no longer remember. Each interaction felt intimidating. Every member Arby introduced was older, taller, and had that certain mature air adults had. Jin wasn't used to talking to such people as equals. He had quickly started to feel out of place and wondered if he really belonged there.

That was, until Arby introduced him to Magnus.

"My name is Magnus, and I like hamburgers and turtles," he'd said in a squeaky voice. He was a young Norwegian boy with parted brown hair who happened to be a year younger than Jin. He had been recruited by Arby not too long ago as well.

"My name is Jin, and I like VR and movies," Jin responded.

Magnus was the only person there shorter than Jin. It was a breath of fresh air to have somebody his age there. He could tell Magnus felt the same way. When they shook hands for the first time, it felt like a load of weight had just been taken off both of their shoulders.

When Jin's first day of practice actually began, it was the most intense physical activity he had ever done. Drills, sprints, bodyweight calisthenics, stretching, and sparring were all part of the daily routine. He felt himself constantly falling behind. Most of the athletes moved swiftly and thoughtlessly. It was clear that they'd done this hundreds of times before.

By the halfway mark, Jin already felt his body collapsing. He couldn't keep up. He was pushed to a point that he didn't think possible. It was almost embarrassing, being the weak kid that those serious athletes had to train with.

However, he wasn't alone. Magnus was struggling just as much, if not more so, than Jin. "How is this even possible," Magnus repeatedly whined in a distraught voice.

In fact, for just about every exercise, Magnus always seemed to be just barely a step behind Jin. But in the eyes of all the older athletes, they were probably both just beginners.

The two found support in each other, trying their best together to keep up with the rest. They found themselves sticking together like magnets. One could never get too far without the other eventually gravitating to the other. Without Magnus, Jin didn't know how he could've possibly made it through that first practice.

Every session became like this. They were the two kids always just trying their best. Arby gradually recruited more and more kids their age to the club—he wanted to begin fostering his next generation of students. However, none of them became as close as Jin and Magnus did.

Eventually, Ethan was recruited as well. Perhaps Jin's recommendation had an impact, but regardless, Ethan's promising results spoke for themselves. Ethan and Magnus became just as close, and soon the trio was formed. They were inseparable. And not only was their bond unlike any of the other kids, but their progress shined as well. They climbed through regional rankings and were able to outclass any of the gym's other students their age.

Jin unquestionably grew the fastest. After one year at the club, he was already blowing through whatever exercise Coach Arby threw his way. The routine that he once couldn't even survive half of eventually felt like a warm-up, and he felt himself craving more.

He was the first among the kids to challenge one of the older students to a spar. Everyone watched. It was almost like a revolutionary moment for the younger students: one of their very own was about to step into a battle with the giants once thought to be untouchable. And although Jin lost, it was closer than anybody expected.

Arby had kept a close eye on the three but saw especially great potential in Jin. He put extensive effort into pushing him further and further. Some of the younger students were jealous at the attention Jin was getting, but many others looked up to him as an example of what they could potentially be.

Nobody at that gym looked up to Jin as much as Magnus. They had started off on a somewhat even playing field, but Jin had risen to a completely different level. Magnus idolized Jin as the pinnacle of success among his peers. "I have to work harder to be like Jin," he would often say.

Jin liked the attention, and, in his young mind, he couldn't help but develop somewhat of an ego. And as he developed his fighting, expectations grew from his coach, his parents, and especially Magnus. And eventually, when those expectations crumbled away, so did the pride that he had built.

CHAPTER 9

Marinated beef was all Jin wanted to be happy. Once it was ready, he stuffed the bulgogi into his mouth. He coughed as the sizzling meat seared the roof of his mouth, but it was still too delicious not to enjoy.

Ethan laughed. "Bro, chill out. That meat's not going anywhere"

"I don't care," Jin whimpered meekly. "Nationals is only a few days away. We need to eat now so that we have stored energy for the big day."

"He's right, how can you savor the meat if you eat it all in an instant?" Mrs. Song chimed in. She was the Korean grandmother who owned the Korean barbeque restaurant. Her kids had grown up in Bezo, but all moved to New York to start their own families. She preferred to work hands-on at the restaurant. The boys ate there often enough to know her personally.

Suddenly, Jin received a text from Char. *Let's do something. Where are you?*

"Hey, is it okay if Charlotte comes?"

Ethan grinned. "Hey, hey, I knew y'all have been getting close lately, but I didn't know y'all were *this* close."

Jin opened his mouth to speak before stopping himself. Normally Jin would object, but now that he thought about it, it was true that he hadn't developed many relationships this close in a long time. They'd hung out quite a bit since he gave her a crash course on VMA.

"Well, maybe now you can meet her too. She's not as weird as everyone says."

Ethan leaned back into his chair. "You sure?"

"Well, she's not weird to me at least. I think you'll like her."

He shrugged. "Sure, why not."

Jin responded to the text with an invitation and address, and by the time the boys finished their food, Char had arrived. They pulled up an extra chair for her to sit with them.

"So you're the Ethan that Jin always talks about," Char said, resting her head on her hand.

"So you're the Charlotte everyone at school always talks about." Ethan put his head on his hand as well, a mirror image.

Charlotte turned her head, staring into Ethan's eyes. He matched her. Jin was a little taken aback. Ethan wasn't usually this bold around strangers.

She smiled. "I can already tell I'm going to like you."

Ethan grinned in his usual stupid way. "Same."

The boys called Mrs. Song to give Char a menu.

"We already finished our meal, but you can order more," Ethan said. "We'll probably be down for another round of food anyway."

She skimmed through the menu. "I have no idea what any of this is."

The boy shook their heads in unison. "I guess we have to educate you on how to be Asian," Jin said.

However, after a lot of explaining, the two ended up just ordering more bulgogi for her to try.

When they finished their meal, they thanked Mrs. Song and took a walk around town. The sun was down, and the hot Texas day was starting to cool off.

"Hey y'all over there! The two guys and the girl."

The three turned to see two tall boys behind them with slicked-back hair and black jackets. They looked like they had been put together by the same stylist.

One of them smiled. "Looks like we got 'em." He pulled his phone from his pocket and began typing.

Charlotte strutted toward the boy and snatched the phone straight out of his hand. "What the hell do you think you're doing?"

The boy grinned. "Too late. They already know you're here. Y'all are fucked."

Suddenly, other boys began to appear from all directions. Many were holding wooden planks. Behind them, Liam was at the center.

"Finally found you," he said, scowling. He spat on the ground and stretched his neck. "You guys fucked with the wrong person."

Jin's heart sank. He'd heard Liam had a tendency to get violent, but he didn't realize he would target people like this. Beside him, Ethan was biting his lip and spinning around, seemingly scanning the number of boys surrounding them. Char, on the other hand, had barely moved and was glaring at Liam. Her face was nearly expressionless, but based off the trembling of her eyebrows, Jin could tell she was containing her panic.

Liam circled the three, hands stuffed in the pockets of his navy bomber jacket. "I'm sure y'all know what's about to happen, right?" His tone was intense, shuddering with pent-up rage about to boil over.

"Come on, Liam." Ethan said. "What's going on?"

Liam glanced at Ethan before shaking his head. He began to walk, taking his time with every step. He stopped in front of Ethan. The two were now face-to-face; any step forward would cause them to collide. Liam put his hand on Ethan's shoulder, grasping it in a tense grip. "This doesn't concern you. You weren't there. I'd recommend leaving now before I stop being this generous."

"It does concern me." Ethan stood his ground. "Especially when you're so generous as to bring a whole gang to pick on just two people."

Liam's grip tightened. "Don't make me hurt you too."

Ethan clenched his fist, moved in a flash. *Crack.* Liam flew back, trembling backward into the boys behind him.

Shockingly, Ethan had thrown the first punch. Then all hell broke loose.

Liam's waiting crew was now flinging themselves forward. Ethan dodged and swung back. Jin blocked and turned to Charlotte. She was pepper spraying a boy when another snuck up from behind and smacked her back with a plank. She shrieked and dropped to her knees.

Fuck. Jin pushed the boy in front of him and ran to Charlotte. Suddenly, a boy snapped a plank across Jin's knee. He plunged forward, cheek rubbing on the coarse concrete. He groaned in agony. Suddenly, a kick to the gut. The boy was continuing to beat Jin on the ground.

oomf. oomf.

With every blow, Jin could feel his breath being shoved out of his stomach. His mind was spinning. He looked up and saw Ethan through the bodies of Liam's thugs, holding his own and fighting multiple at once.

"stop. stop. break it up, now." An adult's voice yelled through the violence. It was the police.

CHAPTER 10

Jin had been staring at the plain white walls in his father's office for nearly an hour now. His mind was blank. After the deafening screams of the skirmish, the police station's silence felt uneasy. Char lived close to the fight site, so she had been escorted home. Ethan was lying face down on the small, black couch across from Jin, burying his head in a cushion. They hadn't spoken a word since they arrived. They were waiting for Ethan's family to pick him up.

Suddenly the door opened. An enormous man in a suede overcoat and parted coffee-colored hair walked into the office. Jin felt his muscles tense up with an icy chill. It was Ethan's father, Mr. Miller.

The two boys sprang up, as if the man's very presence commanded it. Somehow, the room seemed even more silent than it was before.

He turned toward Jin and sighed. "I knew it."

"Dad, stop. Jin had nothing to do with this. I was the one who—"

"I didn't even say his name. The fact that you already know what's wrong before I say anything proves my point."

Ethan glared with his jaw clenched.

Despite the silence, the tension felt as if it could snap at any moment.

"I'm starting to get fed up with you, kid." Mr. Miller's deep voice echoed through the room, filling it with its weight. "Nothing good comes from you being involved. I can't let you ruin my son's life like this. Stop seeing him."

Jin nodded. He couldn't bring himself to say a word. There was that same feeling: the inescapable dread that he was right.

"Why are you always like this Dad?" Ethan ripped the words out of his mouth, voice throbbing with emotion. "It's always about us. Always trying to be on top without any regard for anybody else. I've never seen you look at things from another perspective in my whole life. Everyone who's been dealt a bad hand in life is just trash to you."

Ethan was panting now. His shoulders were tense, and his eyes were glued forward.

Mr. Miller paused as if he was surprised, but his face held the same snide expression. "This is what I mean. Your pity for these scum is making you soft. It's no wonder. You just don't know better. I see I've failed to teach you things correctly."

Ethan was starting to gleam with anger. It was written all over his face. Jin was stunned in place. He'd never seen Ethan like this before. Despite all these years, it was like he was seeing a side of Ethan that had remained hidden all this time.

"I suppose this may be my fault," Mr. Miller said. "I was too lenient. I wanted to let you play around, but you've lost yourself in it. Wasting time on worthless people and meaningless projects."

"I don't want to become like you. Living only for yourself and your ego. Everything you do comes down to that. Your career. Your reputation. Even your family. You only maintain it to satisfy your pride. You married a young, foreign girl to prove you could realize your disgusting fantasies. You groom your children into copies of you to prove that you can nurture success. All this just to wear your family like a medal. Just to—"

Smack.

Jin flinched. The sudden pop rang through his ears like a booming jolt of energy. Ethan had been slapped with so much force that the air seemed to part around him. But somehow, he stood his ground without falling over. His face was already beginning to swell. His deadpan expression was in a daze, as if he was paralyzed.

"I think it's time to go home now." Mr. Miller's low voice was unusually mellow. He grabbed Ethan's arm and yanked him toward the door. Ethan's father gazed at Jin one more time as he passed. "Don't interact with my son again until you've become competent."

And just like that, they were gone.

Jin collapsed onto the ground. He could feel his body getting heavier and the cold tile pressed against his skin. He let himself stay like this for a while.

When he got up, his body was exhausted as if he had just finished a workout. It was nearly midnight now.

Where the fuck is my dad?

Jin exited through the door and down a hallway. Men and women in suits were still rushing through, ignoring Jin. He wandered around the offices before eventually finding his father at the edge of the lobby, chatting with a young woman officer with brown hair. Jin approached the two, but they didn't seem to notice.

Nearly ten minutes passed before they even acknowledged Jin's presence a few feet away from them. His father turned and smiled gently.

"Oh, Jin! Just in time, I was about to grab you." He turned back to the woman. "We'll continue this conversation tomorrow morning."

The woman nodded and kept a straight face, but she seemed to be disappointed.

Mr. Yi led Jin out of the police station and to his car. Jin took a seat, and his father plopped down a folder that had way too many pieces of paper shoved inside.

"Hold onto that for the ride. Don't bend it up, though. I'll be in trouble if you ruin it."

Jin's father was smiling, but through the folds on his forehead, eyebags, and unshaven stubble, Jin could tell he was stressed. It was what his dad usually did—joke and ignore the fact that he was hiding confidential info. It wasn't a shock to Jin that his father didn't even seem to mind his son getting in a fight.

His father closed the door and leaned forward to enter the address into the car's navigation. He had the latest craze these days—a self-driving car. Simply typing in an address was all it took to begin a trip with the vehicle. Jin thought they were cool, but if he were being honest, he didn't really care much for them. He didn't drive anyway.

Soon, the two were on their way home. Jin looked out the window to stare at the city. Most of it was too dark to see, with the few buildings visible from the moonlight or streetlamps flashing by. The gentle hum of the car was calming, and soon he was drifting away.

* * *

Jin hated responsibility. He hated being the reason something crashed down. It revealed his shortcomings and his inability to perform. However, it was unavoidable. Just by being in a relationship with other people, he found himself thrown into overwhelming responsibility. And because of this unwanted responsibility, things always ended up being his fault. His fault Ethan was stuck babysitting a bum. His fault Char was caught by the police. His fault his dad had to wring in his own son. His fault his mom died.

The day it happened, Jin had already been VR Fighting for a year and a half. He didn't want to do anything else. VMA became ingrained into his personal identity. It defined how he saw himself: he labeled himself as a VR Fighter more than he did a student.

So when Jin's mother wanted him to continue math tutoring, something inside of him rejected it. It felt useless, like a distraction from what he really wanted to be doing.

So one day when the school bell rang, he ignored his usual text from his mom. She always scheduled his tutoring right after school but he wanted to act dumb. It was just like the day he started VMA.

Instead, he went to Ethan's classroom. Together, the boys went down to the art room, where they usually snuck out the window and through the hole under the fence. Soon, they were outside, and texting their friends to meet at the playground. Jin got another message but didn't read it.

The boys proceeded to Coach Arby's gym to get in some more training. When they arrived, Jin got another notification. He had started to wonder what took so long, considering how often his mom texted. He checked his phone and saw that it wasn't actually his mom who texted him, but his dad. All the message said was: *Jin, come to school right now.*

Jin didn't know what to make of this, so he excused himself from his friends and ran back to school. When he arrived, he didn't know what he was looking at. A car had rolled over onto its side; its bottom half had been crushed. A bit away, another car had its front half completely gone, and what was remaining had been blackened with ash. A large number of people were surrounding the vehicles, seemingly in shock.

He scanned through the crowd to find his dad and found him by the flipped-over car with police officers. As he approached them, he could hear their conversation and could see that his dad was crying.

"We're not exactly sure what happened. It must've been some sort of bug or malfunction with the car's software," the officer said.

Mr. Yi nodded. This was Jin's first time seeing his dad cry; he was normally the silent, gentle type.

"Where's Mom?" Jin asked.

His father turned his head. He could barely bring himself to look at his own son.

"She's…gone," he said.

Jin turned toward the cars, recognized his mom's, and finally realized what had happened. The emotions came all at once, and he didn't know how to act. He wanted to run and scream, but nothing came out. He just stared at the cars and sank down onto his knees.

He stayed home from school the next day. And the next. And the next. Soon a week had passed, and he still felt the same. His father didn't bother him. Perhaps because he knew how much pain he was going through. Or perhaps he was overwhelmed with pain himself.

During this time, he was alone in his room. Nobody was there to tell him to get up. Or to go to school. Or to talk to his friends.

What eventually dragged him out of bed was VMA. After a month away, it called for him. After everything else was stripped away, for a boy his age, VMA was all he had left.

But it frightened him. How could he go back to that sport after all that'd happened? But it was also what she would've wanted for Jin. It was the part of him that she supported most—the thing she was most hopeful of. He couldn't quit now.

But he got worse. He couldn't keep up with the progress he was making before. And as his competition results became poorer, he had nobody to blame other than himself. How could he let himself fall off? Wasn't this what he chose to continue? He left behind everything, just to become a loser?

He became a different person. He could no longer bring himself to act charismatic around his peers at the VR gym.

The one who caught on most was Magnus. When the idol he looked up to was no more, his own identity took a hit. He eventually left Arby's club, only to reappear years later as a national champion.

Jin couldn't believe he was still dwelling on this. He felt stupid. *So, so stupid.*

Jin opened his eyes and woke up in the car's passenger seat in a sweat.

"We're home," his father said.

CHAPTER 11

Nationals was finally here.

Jin stood in front of the Austin tournament location. It was a long convention center with glass windows and steel pillars. Every region had their own competition site that players would connect through. If two competitors from different regions were paired together (most matches were across two different regions), then both parties would remotely connect to an online VR room.

He took a deep breath and felt the morning breeze. It was nine in the morning. The last few months had been for this. Physically, Jin felt fine. But he felt lonely. Ever since the police incident, Ethan and Char had grown a bit distant under their parents' influence. If it weren't for that, Jin and Ethan probably would've entered the convention center together.

When he mustered the courage, Jin entered the building alone. He followed the signs through the confusing hallways and found the sign-in desk by the entrance to the competition hall.

Once signed in, he pushed his way through the doors. Inside were dozens of VR stations scattered throughout the hall, and a second-floor balcony for spectators. Upstairs was also a waiting room and warm-up zone for athletes.

However, Jin barely had any time to warm up before the competition started up. The tournament bracket was released on a large monitor in the center of the arena. Jin's heart sank. His Round One pairing was Ethan.

When he arrived at their designated VR station, Ethan looked exhausted. He hadn't looked like that in years. They made eye contact, but no words were said for what seemed like minutes. It was Ethan who broke the silence. "Good luck, man."

"You too." For some reason, Jin couldn't look him in the eye.

When they hooked on their headsets and entered the VR room, the two boys found themselves staring at each other again, but this time alone. Nobody else in the space to distract them. The typically blank scent of VR for some reason smelled bitter today.

Ethan used the spear and preferred balanced, careful movements from a distance. The two had sparred countless times, and Jin knew him well. When they trained, it was back and forth, but Jin knew that Ethan could win whenever he wanted to. He already knew how this was going to play out.

The familiar VMA announcer began the countdown.

Three, two, one... GO!

Ethan was the first to move. He thrusted forward. Jin dodged to the right, but the spear followed, scratching his leg.

Ethan reeled back before thrusting again. Jin dodged left but was hit again. Ethan was predicting his movements.

Jin switched gears. His defense wasn't working, so he had to attack. Jin suddenly closed the distance and prepared a swipe.

Suddenly, a kick to the stomach. Ethan had predicted that too.

No matter what Jin tried, Ethan was always a step ahead. He knew exactly where Jin would dodge, shield, and attack.

The exchanges slowly started to feel the same to Jin. He started to sink, once more, into the dark blue space of his mind. His body moved on its own like a machine. He could tell it had become even easier for Ethan to read his moves. Jin didn't care enough to change his attacking pattern. Or maybe he did care. Maybe that was what he was just telling himself.

Every time he took damage, he felt tension build up in his heart accompanied by a tiny voice whispering *whatever*. His senses began to dull, as if his body knew he wouldn't need them anyway. He was going to lose. It was hopeless. Jin was completely outclassed.

What else did he expect? Did he think he would actually do well in such a high-profile event? If anything, maybe it was a good thing that Ethan had a comfortable first round.

The score was currently 48–13 for Ethan. Jin's mind spun with justifications. He felt sick. His head spun. He wanted to leave.

Until suddenly, Jin landed a clean swipe to Ethan's shoulder. Jin's attention spiked. He swiped again, and again, and again. A combo. Ethan fell back.

38–13.

Jin blinked and took a breath. He felt dragged out of his mind for a moment. He found himself running in again. He wound up for another strike. Ethan shielded, but it was broken by Jin's shieldbreaker.

Ethan stumbled. Jin aimed for his knees.

Smack.

He kept going. Kept swinging. Kept punching. Kept kicking. Ethan was taking it. A glimmer of hope. All those justifications just a few minutes ago, and now none of those were on his mind. Was he being selfish? No, this was competition. *This is the attitude you're supposed to have.*

It felt good. Jin wouldn't admit it to himself, but he desperately wanted to cling on to the thread of hope laid out before him. He kept attacking. Whatever Ethan chose to defend with, Jin somehow saw it coming. He was barely thinking, but his mind always seemed to know the answer.

He swung and swung and swung until he realized: Ethan was letting him win.

Jin stopped. He stepped back and breathed. The score was 12–7, close to even. He couldn't win like this. *Ethan can't do this.* He wanted to call out to Ethan. Beg him not to throw away this opportunity. After all that time preparing for this competition, Ethan couldn't do this for someone Jin's level.

Jin stood still. Ethan wasn't coming after him. Why wasn't he? He could end it any time he wanted.

Ethan's expression looked pained, and Jin hated it. It was his fault again—he was the reason Ethan was so conflicted. Shame took over Jin's body. His knees shook, and he didn't want to move. The two stood there for what felt like hours. They looked into each other's eyes. Jin wondered what facial expression he was making right then.

Jin lowered his guard. Ethan's expression dropped. He knew exactly what he was trying to say. Ethan shook his head, but Jin signaled him forward. Ethan kept shaking and looked down. He dropped to his knees.

Jin closed his eyes. He couldn't bear to see his best friend like this. Everything went quiet again.

When he finally opened them, a punch was coming straight for his face.

And then, it was over. Ethan had won.

CHAPTER 12

The athletes' waiting room was now filled with the losers from the first round. The disappointment looming in the air was practically tangible. Jin was one of those losers. He reclined on a couch against the wall, staring at the ceiling. Thoughts were darting back and forth through his head, but he couldn't understand a single one.

It felt like a lot of time had passed on the couch, but he couldn't tell for sure.

Suddenly, a tap on his shoulder. He turned his head. It was Coach Arby.

Jin sat up and faked a smile.

Arby smiled back and sat next to him.

"Hey," Arby said.

"Hey."

Arby paused, choosing his words carefully. "So son," he started, "how are you feeling about the competition?"

Jin was more or less expecting something like this. "Not amazing," he responded.

Coach nodded. "I understand. Is something on your mind?"

"What do you mean?"

"Well, it just seems like you're lost in thought."

"Aren't I usually like this?"

Coach paused again. "Jin, have you…thought about your future?"

A pivot. The word sank deep. It just occurred to Jin that out of all these years with Arby, this was the first time he had asked this question. In fact, Arby was practically the only one who hadn't already asked this.

"A little bit."

"So… Are you on track for that future?"

Jin squirmed in his seat uncomfortably. He didn't respond.

"Jin, is this what you want to be doing for the rest of your life?"

Jin looked up. "What are you trying to say?"

Coach Arby bit his lip. He looked at the wall and sighed. "It's tough, Jin. I just want to look out for you. I know it's tough, and I know there's a lot on your shoulders. Are you sure you want VMA to be one of them? Where you are right now…do you think you can get where you want? It may be better for your future to do something else. You still have time, you're so young. You can probably pick up something that the algorithm likes. Live a comfortable life without the stress. Without the expectations I know you put on yourself."

Jin didn't know what his face looked like in that moment, but he knew his pain was clearly visible. He didn't disagree with Coach, but he didn't know what to say.

He took his time before responding, and Coach Arby waited patiently for him.

"Thank you."

Arby nodded. "I'll give you some space." He patted Jin's back and left.

When the door shut behind Arby, Jin collapsed back onto the couch. His heart ached. He felt alone.

He lay down again, this time facedown into the couch's cushion. He had trouble breathing, but he didn't care. He simply wallowed, feeling the pain in his chest grow. It spread, squeezing his limbs and hands. It consumed him. He lost track of everything else—the tight sensation was all he could experience.

Suddenly, an announcement blared out of the speaker in the room:

"Seokjin Yi, please report to the sign-in table immediately."

He rolled over. He didn't feel like getting up, but he forced himself onto his feet. He wasn't sure what the tournament organizers would want; they'd never done anything like this with him before.

He stumbled forward, the tightness in his heart making him feel weak, but he eventually made his way out of the door and through the hallway. He passed the competition hall, clinging to the wall so as to not interact with anyone, and reached the sign-in desk, where a few officials were sitting next to each other. They were three tall, balding men and a woman with short, tidy hair.

When Jin approached them, the four turned and looked at him. "Have a seat," one of the men said, signaling toward a chair.

Jin complied, pulling up a chair across the table from the officials.

The woman spoke first. "Here's what's going on. Your last opponent dropped out of the competition."

Jin's eyes widened. He nearly sprung up to his feet. "What? Ethan?"

She nodded. "So, because he's no longer competing, he will not be the one advancing to the next round. You now have the opportunity to take his place."

Jin's mouth dropped open. He was speechless. How could Ethan do this? He started to feel angry. *Why? Why? Why is Ethan letting his emotions get the better of him?*

It was all Jin's fault. He sank into his chair. Another wave of guilt circulated through him.

He took a deep breath, trying to compose himself in front of these officials. "So who's my next opponent then?"

The woman looked forward, deep into Jin's eyes. "Magnus Andersen."

CHAPTER 13

Jin dragged his feet as he walked through the competition hall. Seeing the VR stations scattered throughout the room made his heart ache again. He was thrust back into this hell.

Round Two wasn't scheduled to start till half an hour later, and Jin was restless. He circled around the competition hall. Emotions were running rampant in his head, but he tried his best to quiet them, to focus for the next match.

His next match was against *Magnus*. He was most certainly going to lose. There was no other possible outcome. It was *Ethan* who was supposed to fight Magnus. He might've had a chance. Magnus was among the best in the nation, but Ethan was among the best in the state, with a solid footing at the national level. Jin, on the other hand, was a nobody.

Why was he still here? Luck. That was the only reason. He felt ashamed. He should know his place. Why was he wasting everyone's time? Why would he waste Magnus' time?

He should drop out. Ethan did it, so why couldn't he? That was the most respectful thing to do. Jin clenched his fist and turned around to tell the officials at the sign-in desk that he was going to quit, but Char was suddenly in his way.

"Where are you going?" she asked.

"I'm going to drop out."

She seemed startled. "What the fuck? Why?"

"Look." Jin broke eye contact. "You probably didn't see, but I don't deserve to still be in."

"No, no." She shook her head. "I saw everything."

"Then you should understand."

She shook her head. "Don't you want to fight, though?"

"Why does that matter?"

"Because that's the most important part."

"Why should I when it only hurts other people? Me being here ruined Ethan's shot at nationals. Me being here just wasted time. Even Coach Arby has had enough of babysitting me. I'm not helping anyone by—"

Char grabbed Jin's collar and yanked him closer. Her face looked tense, and her eyes were unstable, as if she was about to cry. "Jin…I…I…"

Her voice sounded frail, and her hands began to shake. "I want you to think about yourself. You keep placing the blame on yourself for everything, but they're just excuses to keep you from thinking about what you need."

Jin looked down, heart pounding. "I just don't want to be selfish."

"No, it's not selfish." She was screaming now. "Jin, no matter what happens, no matter who comes and goes, the only person who can be there for you is yourself. I know you're scared, but the only person responsible for your own well-being is *you*."

Jin couldn't look her in the eyes. His knees felt weak. If she wasn't grabbing onto him so tight, he probably would've collapsed onto the ground.

"Look at yourself," she continued. "I know so much shit has happened, but you can't let it destroy your life like this. I know you love this sport so much, so home in on that."

"I don't love it… I just have to. Without it, I have nothing…" Jin didn't know what to do. His heart burned to continue VR Fighting, to honor the opportunities given to him. But he couldn't follow through. Every time he either hurt someone or let down those who believed in him. If his mom could see how little progress he'd made, she'd be heartbroken. He had desperately hung onto the hope that he could prove himself wrong, but he'd done nothing but make things worse.

"I've wasted what everyone has sacrificed for me," he muttered.

"Stop it, Jin!" Char raised her arm and slapped him with all the power she could muster. Jin's head whipped to the side, stinging pain running across his skin.

"Don't do it for them, do it for yourself. Don't feel guilty for being yourself."

Jin nodded. He gently removed her hand from his collar and held it in his for a moment before letting go. He walked away.

"Jin," Charlotte called.

He turned around.

"You have something amazing here. I don't care what Ethan, your coach, or anybody in the audience says. I've told you this before, but I've wanted what you have for so, so long. I can't stand to see you in pain because of it. You don't have to win. You don't have to prove anything to anyone. Just go play."

He nodded and turned back around.

Round Two competitors were called up at 11:00 a.m. sharp. They had fifteen minutes to report to the main competition hall and hook into their VR stations. When Jin arrived to the designated station, Magnus was already waiting for him. His long hair was tied back, and his hands were buried in the pockets of his track pants.

"I didn't expect to run into you here," Magnus said.

"Me either."

"Why did Ethan drop out?"

"I don't know. He didn't tell me."

Magnus sighed. There was an awkward silence for a moment before he continued. "You know, Jin, I don't hate you. I'm just disappointed."

The words stung, but Jin couldn't think of a response. He already felt emotionally drained.

Magnus waited for a few moments, until he realized that no response was coming.

"Tsk." He pulled his hands out of his pockets and stretched his back. "You could've been so much more. You didn't deserve this."

Jin just nodded. At this point, everyone's words felt the same to him. He didn't care anymore.

When the announcer gave the signal, the two hooked up to the VR station. After the familiar countdown, the match began.

The two got in their stance. Magnus also used the iron rod, but he was nearly a head taller.

Magnus bounced around, slipping in and out of attacking distance. He was clearly in no rush. The two poked with small jabs and kicks, but neither player really committed to anything.

Suddenly, Magnus approached with a swipe high. Jin shielded. Magnus stepped in again with a swipe low. Shielded.

Jin stumbled back, but Magnus retreated, shoulders relaxed. He seemed too lazy to follow-up on his attacks.

Magnus slowly put his weight onto his back foot before lunging powerfully into a kick. Jin put up his shield, but it shattered. He'd been hit with a shieldbreaker.

50–42.

Jin knew exactly what had happened. It was clear—he'd shielded twice in a row, so he probably had tendency to shield. Magnus' SB confirmed it. But it didn't matter. He was going to lose anyway. Why worry? Why linger on his mistakes?

Jin took a few steps and took a breath. But Magnus moved in again with a kick low.

It was clearly a feint. He was trying to bait a reaction. Jin stepped in with a counterattack.

Magnus stumbled a bit, but quickly regained his balance and retreated. He shook his head, startled but collecting his focus.

He approached again.

A jab. A straight. Another feint high—

Jin swerved and smacked him with a counter.

Again.

A swipe. A straight. A fei—

Another easy counter.

Magnus faltered, tension clearly building in his eyes. He swiped again. This time, it was rushed. Jin just swerved and hit him with a riposte. He felt his bar digging into Magnus' skin.

It felt good. It felt natural.

Magnus was getting frustrated. He kept running in with an attack, but Jin could see right through it. Everything seemed clear to him. All his movements seemed so obvious. Was this really the national champion that everyone looked up to?

Soon, it was 34–40. Jin was in the lead. Magnus backed off, face red with irritation. He probably realized that attacking wasn't working, so he switched to defense. Jin straightened his back. He felt good.

He took a breath and realized something. He wasn't in the deep blue of his mind. There wasn't any brain fog, tightness, or distraction. Just him, Magnus, and the fight. He felt exposed, but confident. He'd almost forgotten what it felt like to fight like this. Without the burden of his own mind.

His mind and body felt connected. Through every exchange, he knew exactly what was coming and his body moved accordingly. His mind felt like a computer, able to calculate the correct play with a split-second of observation. He felt smooth and light on his feet. he did every attack, dodge, and shield relaxed but decisively. He wasn't thinking about what would happen next, and he didn't care.

At 21–38, Magnus started to change. He regained his composure and started playing smarter. Now it was his turn to read Jin, who received a number of hard blows. But Jin wasn't mad. He just played the game.

They evened it out at 20–22 and went back and forth. Jin began to read Magnus' moves again, and Magnus was reading his. This kept going, on and on, back and forth. Jin was focused. He wasn't worried about what would happen, he was only concerned with fighting well.

Jabs, kicks, and strikes were all thrown out. Jin used every trick he knew until finally, it was 5–5. The match point. Whoever got the next point won.

The two circled around each other. Jin's mind raced. Would he thrust forward and try to fit in a feint? Would he jab to try to provoke the counter? Or would he do what Magnus just did and predict Jin's feint?

It didn't matter. Jin's body lunged forward on its own. He faked high. Magnus read that and prepared for a shot low. However, instead, Jin threw his body weight down and stomped Magnus' foot. He yelped.

That was it. Magnus' health bar fell to zero. Jin was victorious.

CHAPTER 14

When Jin unhooked his headgear, he saw Magnus sitting with his hands gripping his knees. He was staring at the floor, arms trembling. Never did Jin think he would ever see Magnus before him, frustrated like this. It felt strange, but he didn't mind.

He reached his hand out to Magnus. "That was a good match." The words felt good coming out of his mouth. He hadn't said something like this in years.

Magnus glanced up and reluctantly shook his hand, but then stormed out without saying a word.

That was it. He just beat *the* Magnus Andersen. He took a breath. The chilly AC tickled his nose, flowing through nostrils and filling his mouth. Goosebumps appeared on his arms. Was air always this clear?

Once outside the competition hall, Jin stood in front of the door of the athletes' waiting room. He didn't know what to do. Normally, at this point in the competition, he'd go home. But now here he was, waiting for the third round.

Abruptly, a small noise. He turned and saw Char darting toward him. She jumped forward and threw her weight into a tackle, knocking Jin down.

"JIN! JIN!" she panted, gasping for air.

He smiled back. "You were right."

Saying the words out loud made him realize just how many things she was right about. He felt stupid.

She looked up and smiled back.

Suddenly, Ethan appeared behind her, hair slicked back and one hand in his pocket. "Congratulations," he said in a cheerful voice.

Jin's mouth dropped. He jumped onto his feet and approached his best friend. "Why did you do that?"

"Wha—"

"C'mon, man. *Seriously.*"

Ethan smiled, pulling his hand out of his pocket and folding his arms together. "It felt right."

Jin's lips tightened. "What?"

"At first I felt bad," he said, voice frailer than Jin had ever heard it, as if he didn't want to say it out loud. "And then I felt bad that I was feeling bad. I didn't want to pity you."

"So you decided to drop out?"

Ethan laughed, but it seemed forced. "I don't know… I'm not sure what I was thinking, or if I was thinking at all. I just hated feeling like that. I thought running away and going home would make me feel better, but after I dropped, I couldn't bring myself to leave."

He hesitated a moment before continuing. "Jin, you did something insane today. I think I ended up making the right decision."

Char poked her head from behind Jin's shoulder. "I think so too!"

Jin smiled and looked up. Ethan's dark blue eyes were staring straight into his. There was a certain intensity to his gaze, one that nailed in the message that he meant what he was saying.

"Thank you," Jin responded. He didn't know what else to say, but the look in Ethan's eyes told him that he knew exactly how he felt.

When the next round started, Jin quickly lost to a young fighter from California—but he didn't care. Sure he'd made a pretty solid result with a Round Three finish and a spot in the top 128, but it wasn't just that. He felt satisfied. His mind was clear, as if the weighted fog hanging inside his head had been blown away.

Unsurprisingly, his upset against Magnus was big news. Not for Jin's success, but Magnus' failure. "Magnus' choke threw off the whole bracket," rumors said. Jin didn't mind, though. He didn't seem to mind a lot of things anymore.

* * *

The midnight stars shone through Jin's kitchen window. He liked to keep it open now, hearing the suburban cars drive by and feeling the cool breeze.

The door opened, and Mr. Yi walked inside. His hair was oily with sweat built up throughout the day. "Sorry I'm late, Jin. You know how work is." He pulled up a chair and slung his jacket across the back.

"It's okay."

"I was really surprised when you texted me," his father said with a fake chuckle. He set his bag down on the table and settled into his seat. He seemed stiff as he forced himself down. "You never ask me to talk."

Jin laughed back. "I thought it was about time."

Mr. Yi hesitated before nodding his head. "I'm really happy to hear that."

There was a silence.

"Dad," Jin started. "I want to go to school again."

Mr. Yi flinched, caught a bit off guard. He grabbed a plastic water bottle out of his bag and took a sip before looking back at Jin. His facial expression slowly relaxed. "What happened?"

"I just…" Jin wanted to find the right words before saying them. "I want to set myself back on track. I don't want to continue harming myself and the people around me because of the past."

His father's eyes began to glimmer in the lamp light, as if tears might be starting to form. His lips gently moved into a smile. But this one felt different. For the first time in years, the smile felt genuine. "I'm so proud of you, son."

Jin looked down at the table. He wasn't used to affection like this from his dad.

"You've begun to do something that I could not. Your mom was everything to me, and I have let losing her hold me hostage for three years. However, it looks like you've finally been able to break free."

Despite the strange, vulnerable feeling that his father's words gave him, Jin forced himself to look up.

Mr. Yi let out a sigh of relief, tension visibly leaving his shoulders.

"Welcome home, Jin."